Zacharias Tanee Fomum

PRAYING WITH POWER

Éditions du Livre Chrétien
4, rue du Révérend Père Cloarec
92400 Courbevoie France
editionlivrechretien@gmail.com

First edition by Vantage Press, New York.
2000 edition under licence from the author,
by Crossroads Communications
C13 CoziHom, 251 Pali Hill, Bandra,
Mumbai 400 050 India

ISBN 0-533-09575-1
Library of Congress Catalog Card No.: 91-90888
Praying with Power
(With Christ in the School and Ministry of Praying)

All Biblical quotations, unless otherwise noted, are from the English Revised Standard Version of the Bible

Printed by :

Editions du livre chrétien

4, rue du Révérend Père Cloarec

92400 Courbevoie - FRANCE

Tél : (33) 9 52 29 27 72

Email : editionlivrechretien@gmail.com

Cover :

Jacques Maré

I lovingly dedicate this book to

JOSEPH TANYI MBAFOR

my brother, my son, my student,
my colleague and my fellow worker,
with gratitude and in glorious expectation.

TABLE OF CONTENTS

1INTRODUCTION 11

Part 1: THE PRAYER MINISTRY OF JESUS (1) 15
1. Prayer 16
2. Prayerlessness 20
3. At twelve in the house of prayer 23
4. The house of prayer 29
5. Eighteen crucial years 33
6. Baptized and praying 41
7. Lord, open the heavens! 47
8. God before man 56
9. Undistracted 67
10. The whole night 78
11. Alone in the midst of others 85
12. Praying and transfigured 91
13. Thanksgiving and worship 102
14. The battle for missions 109

Part 2 : JESUS'S SCHOOL OF PRAYING 119
15. The one thing that needed to be taught 120
16. Jesus gave them what to say 124
17. Jesus taught them spiritual contact 143
18. Jesus taught them by his own life that what a person is, is critically important to the impact that his prayers will produce 149
19. Jesus taught them that the first priority in prayer is to pray that God's name be hallowed 161
20. Jesus taught them that the second priority in prayer is to pray that God's kingdom should come 167
21. Jesus taught them that the third priority in prayer is to pray that God's will be done on earth as it is in

heaven 171
22. Jesus taught them to pray for their personal needs
the place of personal needs in the prayer life 177
23. Jesus taught them to pray for their personal needs
asking for daily bread and other daily needs 182
24. Jesus taught them to pray for their personal needs
asking for forgiveness 190
25. Jesus taught them to pray for their personal needs
forgiveness granted 194
26. Jesus taught them to pray for their personal needs
lead us not into temptation! 198
27. Jesus taught them to pray for their personal needs
deliver us from the evil one 204
28. Jesus taught them that it was necessary to believe
before they saw 208
29. Jesus taught them to pray in his name 218
30. Jesus taught them the indispensable humility 224

Part 3 : THE PRAYER MINISTRY OF JESUS (2) 233

31. Four days in intercession 234
32. The father who always hears 240
33. The violent praying of the Lord Jesus 245
34. Praying in Gethsemane 250
35. Praying from the cross 255
36. Praying, from the throne! from His glory! 259
37. His disciples now! 265
38. Rend the heavens, o Lord! 268

FOREWORD

This book, "PRAYER WITH POWER" is the fifth, in the series: "The Prayer Life." The books in this series that have already been written are:

1. The Way of Victorious Praying
2. The Ministry of Fasting
3. The Art of Intercession
4. The Practice of Intercession
5. **Prayer With Power**
6. Moving God Through Prayer
7. Practical Spiritual Warfare Through Prayer
8. The Ministry of Praise and Thanksgiving
9. The Ministry of Supplication
10. Waiting on the Lord in Prayer

The first forth books have been published in hard cover by Vantage Press, 516 West 34th Street, New York 10001, U.S.A.

The fifth book in the series is in your hands. May the Lord bless you abundantly as you read it, and may He lead you into deeper experience with Christ in the school of prayer with power.

If you have been blessed through the reading of this book, you may want to read the preceding ones and perhaps help some one else to read them. Won't you do so? God bless you abundantly!

Yaounde, 28th April, 1990.

Zacharias TANEE FOMUM,
P.O. Box 6090,
Yaounde - Cameroon.

INTRODUCTION

INTRODUCTION

I have always known that the Lord Jesus prayed. Recently I have been meditating from the Gospel of Luke. It is then that I was taken aback by the prayer life of the Lord Jesus. His whole life was taken up by prayer. He lived in the Father's presence. His life was spent in prayer. He occasionally came away from praying to carry out some task that was assigned to Him by the Father, and went back to prayer as soon as the task was completed.

I have been deeply moved by the quality and quantity of the Lord's prayers. He just prayed. It is obvious from the way He prayed that He understood that everything depended on prayer.

I am convinced that the Lord Jesus understood the true value of prayer. That value was reflected by how much He prayed. I am also now more aware that through a special activity of the Enemy, the Church has been blinded from seeing prayer as the Father sees it and seeing prayer as the Son saw it. This blindness seems total in some quarters and is certainly partial in all others.

As a people of God in the city of Yaounde, our eyes are beginning to be opened to the importance of prayer. This has resulted in individual prayer crusades prayer crusades of two, four, six people and prayer crusades of the House Churches. This has also resulted in the seven prayer chains that are scattered in this city where people are keeping prayer vigils round the clock twenty-four hours a day, seven days a week.

We believe that this is only the beginning. Our eyes are only partially open because there is yet only limited burden that leads to heart-rending before God and heaven-storming in prayer. We plead with the Lord that He should open our eyes so that we might see more clearly the critical importance of prayer. We also pray that He should open our eyes to how late the hour is. We pray that He should teach us and enable us to pour out our all in prayer, to convert sleeping time into prayer time; to convert every available minute into prayer time. We pray also that He should enable us to handle the practical aspects of prayer to the best advantage; for a well-equipped but poorly organized army might yet suffer serious loss.

There are other things that ought to have been included in this book. We have thought it best to leave some of them for the subsequent books that, by God's grace, will follow.

The substance of these messages was first given to leaders of House Churches in the city of Yaounde and around. At the time of delivery it was not intended that these messages would become a book, but the Lord has willed it to be so. As a companion volume to this book is the next book in this series, The Phenomenon of Prayer. Both series of messages were given at the same time. We would have liked to make both into one book, but there was a problem of size. If you have read this message and been blessed, you will want to read the next book in the series. You will also find that you need the material in the first four books to come to grips with the themes of prayer, fasting and intercession.

A book on prayer is not a novel. It cannot be read with ease or in one go. It has to be taken in small bites. I suggest that you should first read the book quickly through and then come back for a slower reading in which you take a bite at a time. I have established the habit of having a good book on prayer on the table or near the bed. I always carry one with me. As I read small portions from books like those by E.M. Bounds, I am stirred to pray. You too might find the habit beneficial. You may find that one of the books or some of the books in this series are a blessing to you.

The Lord was in the Ministry of Praying. He also taught His disciples how to pray. You and I should go and do likewise and we shall indeed be blessed and, above all, the Lord's name shall be glorified.

Amen.

11th July 1989.

PART 1

The Prayer Ministry Of Jesus (1)

1

PRAYER

1. The Lord Jesus had to be in the house of prayer. He had to pray. Prayer was His very life. Everything began and ended in prayer. He prayed before He did things. He prayed while He did things and He prayed for what had been done!
2. The Lord Jesus lived to do His Father's will and that will was received and executed primarily through prayer.
3. When the Lord Jesus entered the temple at the age of twelve, He was already a master at the art of praying; He did not automatically know how to pray. He learned to pray. He spent the first twelve years of His life learning how to do the most important "must" of His life. He was taught to pray by His Father. In order to learn and make rapid progress, He must have given Himself totally to learning how to pray.
4. It is to be expected that the disciple will enrol in the "School of Prayer" that is run by God, spend many years there and from Him learn the art of praying.
5. It is also to be expected that the wise disciple will enrol in the School of Prayer of some advanced saint who has been taught by God to pray and there learn from man how to pray. In that way that saint will supplement what was received in God's School of Prayer with what has been received in Man's School of Prayer and, thereby, make rapid progress.
6. The problem of our day is that there are few, very few who want to pay the price of enrolment in God's School of Prayer.

In addition to this, the Schools of Prayer of men after God's heart are hardly existent.

7. The primary essence of prayer is communion with God.
8. The believer's spirit is his primary school of prayer. It is here that the Holy Spirit dwells and receives from the Father and gives to the believer.
9. Since the spirit of the believer is the place of contact and communion with the Holy Spirit, and since there is no other way by which the believer can enter into communion with God except through the Holy Spirit, we can say that the spirit of the believer is the place where prayer takes place; for there the believer receives God's will and prays it back to the Father from there.
10. The believer who would make progress in the Ministry of Prayer must get rid of every sin in his life. He must be pure in spirit. He must do this, first of all, by being observant and consequently confessing any sin that is manifested in his life, and secondly by labouring to enter into the sanctified life.
11. The preacher who will pray for ten hours and preach for two hours each week will see great things begin to happen in his own life and in the lives of those who listen to his sermons. He will become increasingly filled with God. The dull of hearing will begin to hear; the disobedient will begin to obey; the worldly will begin to find worldly things distasteful; unbelievers will begin to truly understand the gospel and get genuinely saved. A ministry like that of the Lord Jesus will become visible in that place, and God will be glorified.
12. The apostle Paul prayed as if all depended on his prayers and he pleaded with the saints to pray for him as if all depended on their prayers. The combined effects of his praying and theirs was a very fruitful ministry.
13. All work that is not prayed through adequately, several times

over, is actually an activity of the flesh. It will not last. It will bring no reward at the Judgment Seat of the praying Christ.

14. Everyone who wants to do a great work for God must have a clear strategy for praying for everything that he intends to do, well ahead of time. Projects that are to be carried out ten years from today must be soaked in prayer now. It is not enough to pray alone. Prayer partners must be recruited and properly organized into a prayer force.
15. The baptism of Jesus into water was immediately followed by a personal prayer meeting of great intensity on the banks of the Jordan. So mighty was the force of His praying that His prayer tore the sealed heavens and the Holy Spirit gladly came upon Him in bodily form.
16. Anyone who expects any promise of God to be fulfilled in his life or in the life of the Church without sustained co-operation with God in prayer, is mistaken. Anyone who thinks that because he prayed in the past, he can relax at the moment and yet reap the full fruit of God's current move, is self-deceived.
17. God's promises are like pregnancies. Whether or not a healthy child will be born does not only depend on the praying that led to the pregnancy, but even more so on the praying that ensures that the baby grows normally and is protected from disease and premature birth. Even a baby who has grown healthily for nine months in the womb might yet die at delivery. Such a death would be more expensive because of all that has been invested to bring the pregnancy that far. Consequently, the greatest care and the best expertise is required at the point of delivery. The Lord Jesus knew all this and that is why, as He came out of the Jordan, He engaged Himself in violent praying that continued until the Holy Spirit had descended upon Him and remained and His Father had spoken. We too must follow suit and labour in prayer until faith

gives way to sight.

18. It is the prayers of the Lord Jesus that rent the heavens and caused the Holy Spirit to descend upon Him. God was ready to send the Holy Spirit, but how could He descend with a sealed heaven? When the prayers of the Lord Jesus went up, they broke the barrier and down came the Holy Spirit upon Him. He was the first Person to benefit from the Holy Spirit that came down, following the rending of the heaven.
19. An individual believer can cause the heavens to be rent and the power of the Lord to descend on him. You and I are called to do this.
20. And individual believer could cause the heavens to be rent so that the power of the Lord should descend and put to naught the power of Satan that is arrayed against him and against the Church.
21. An individual believer can rend the heavens so that the power of the Lord should descend and bless his assembly, family, town, nation and continent. There is no limit to the blessings which will flow on one and on all if the heavens are rent. Seeing it this way, a single believer can wield limitless power and authority in the overthrow of the kingdom of the evil one.
22. Although individuals can carry out such far-reaching ministry by rending the heavens, God's ultimate purpose is that His total will should be accomplished by the Church working to rend the heavens. May we as individuals and may we as the body rise to the task. Praise the Lord. (Extracts from the first seven chapters.)

2

PRAYERLESSNESS

1. Prayerlessness is the art of putting intercourse with man in the place of intercourse with God.
2. Prayerlessness is the art of putting the secondary issue in the place of the primary issue.
3. Prayerlessness is giving more importance to man than to God.
4. Prayerlessness is the fruit of giving to man the place of God.
5. Prayerlessness is the fruit of thinking that human might and power availeth much.
6. Prayerlessness is the fruit of the philosophy that man is able on his own to know God and serve Him.
7. Prayerlessness is thinking about prayer instead of praying.
8. Prayerlessness is talking about prayer instead of praying.
9. Prayerlessness is preaching about prayer instead of praying.
10. Prayerlessness is teaching on prayer instead of praying.
11. Prayerlessness is writing on prayer instead of praying.
12. Prayerlessness is confessing the sin of prayerlessness and doing nothing after the confession.
13. Prayerlessness is wishing instead of asking.
14. Prayerlessness is planning to pray instead of praying.
15. Prayerlessness is having prayer time on a timetable that is not followed.

16. Prayerlessness is hoping that God knows our needs, instead of telling Him about them.
17. Prayerlessness is planning to pray after the training session, instead of before.
18. Prayerlessness is the art of having prayer in the committee meeting placed as the last item, instead of the first.
19. Prayerlessness is doing a hard day's work, having a good supper, and kneeling by your bedside, to pray? No! To sleep.
20. Prayerlessness is keeping silent at the prayer meeting.
21. Prayerlessness is never praying because someone else always prays before you were able to open your mouth.
22. Prayerlessness is the lot of the person who complains, "Others never let me pray at the prayer meetings. Just as I have organised my thoughts and want to release them to the Lord, behold, someone else prays the very thing I had in my heart and I am stranded."
23. Prayerlessness is the lot of those who have decided that they will not pray until they are able to pray perfectly.
24. The Enemy ensures that normal believers gasp for speech when it is prayer time, but are full of brilliant ideas which they gladly communicate during after-prayer sessions.
25. The Enemy knows the importance of prayer. For that reason, he has attacked 99.9% of the Church with the disease of "prayerlessness".
26. Prayerlessness is often manifested in sleeping during prayer.
27. Prayerlessness is often manifested in the lack of concentration during prayer.
28. Prayerlessness is often manifested in the lack of insistence in prayer.
29. Prayerlessness is often manifested in the lack of boldness during prayer.

30. Prayerlessness and faithlessness go hand in hand.
31. Prayerlessness and sin are partners.
32. Prayerlessness and worldliness are difficult to separate.
33. Prayerlessness and purposelessness are twins.
34. Prayerlessness is the worst sin.
35. God has called prayerlessness to an end. You, too, call it to an end!

3

AT TWELVE IN THE HOUSE OF PRAYER

"Now his parents went to Jerusalem every year at the feast of the Passover. And when he was twelve years old, they went up according to custom; and when the feast was ended, as they were returning, the boy Jesus stayed behind in Jerusalem. His parents did not know it, but supposing him to be in the company they went a day's journey, and they sought him among their kinsfolk and acquaintances; and when they did not find him, they returned to Jerusalem, seeking him. After three days they found him in the temple, sitting among the teachers, listening to them and asking them questions; and all who heard him were amazed at his understanding and his answers. And when they saw him they were astonished; and his mother said to him, 'Son, why have you treated us so? Behold, your father and I have been looking for you anxiously.' And he said to them, 'How is it that you sought me? Did you not know that I must be in my Father's house?' And they did not understand the saying which he spoke to them. And he went down with them and came to Nazareth, and was obedient to them, and his mother kept all these things in her heart" (Luke 2:41-51).

The Lord Jesus and His parents went to Jerusalem together. For them, Jerusalem and the temple were places to visit at fixed intervals, perform rituals and go away gladly. However, for the Lord Jesus, Jerusalem and the temple were different. He lingered there and found His joy and fulfilment there. The parents went homewards and did not find Him. Later on when they found Him, they were surprised that He had treated them so. How did He react? He too was surprised that they sought Him. To Him it was perfectly normal that He ought to have stayed back and not gone back with them. To Him it was but normal that He stayed back in the temple. He found it difficult to understand the fact that they did not understand that He was where He had to be! "How is it that you sought me? Did you not know that I must be in my Father's house?" were words pregnant with meaning.

The temple was His Father's house and it was a must that He be there. Already, at the tender age of twelve, the Lord Jesus was gripped, bound and possessed by the "must" of the musts of His life. There would be other "musts" in His life. For example, He said that the following were "musts":

1. "*I must preach the good news of the kingdom of God to the other cities also; for I was sent for this purpose*" (Luke 4:43).
2. "*And as Moses lifted up the serpent in the wilderness, so must the Son of man be lifted up*" (John 3:14).
3. "*We must work the works of him who sent me, while it is day, night comes, when no one can work*" (John 9:4).
4. "*And I have other sheep, that are not of this fold; I must bring them also, and they will heed my voice. So there shall be one flock, one shepherd*" (John 10:16).
5. "*The Son of man must suffer many things, and be rejected by the elders and chief priests and scribes, and be killed, and on the third day be raised*" (Luke 9:22).

So there were these other "musts" in the life of the Lord Jesus. He was a man under great compulsions. He had time only for that which He had to do. Of these "musts" the most important of them was the one that consumed Him at the age of twelve. It was the first and the most important. Its grip on Him was total and lasted the longest. All the other "musts" in the life of the Lord Jesus were dependent on this "must!"

AT TWELVE IN THE HOUSE OF PRAYER

The Lord Jesus said that it was a must for Him to be in His Father's house. What was His Father's house? The Bible says, "And they came to Jerusalem. And he entered the temple and began to drive out those who sold and those who bought in the temple, and he overturned the tables of the money-changers and the seats of those who sold pigeons; and he would not allow anyone to carry anything through the temple. And he taught, and said to them, 'Is it not written, "*My house shall be called a house of prayer for all the nations*"? *But you have made it a den of robbers*' " (Mark 11:15-17). The prophet Isaiah had said earlier about the temple, "*These I will bring to my holy mountain and make them joyful in my house of prayer; their burnt offerings and their sacrifices will be accepted on my altar; for my house shall be called a house of prayer for all peoples*" (Isaiah 56:7).

The Lord Jesus was thus asking His parents, "How is it that you sought me? Did you not know that I must be in My Father's house? Did you not know that I must be in the house of prayer? Did you not know that if there is one place where I ought to be it ought to be in the house of prayer? Did you not know that if there is one thing that I ought to be doing, I ought to be praying? Did you not know that I have 'musts' in my life and that the 'must' of 'musts,' the 'must' of My life that cannot be negotiated is prayer?"

In thinking, speaking and acting that way, the Lord Jesus allowed us to see the very depths of His commitment to prayer and His personal evaluation of it. It was the very centre, the very life-spring of His life and ministry.

The Lord Jesus expects that we who are His disciples should follow suit. He expects that for the normal believer, the following should be true:

1. That he should have 'musts' in his life and that the greatest 'must,' the 'must of musts,' will be prayer.

2. That the one thing that must always be done will be to pray.
3. That the most frequented place in time should be the place of prayer.
4. That the greatest investment in time should be in prayer.

The Lord Jesus had to be in the House of Prayer. He had to pray. Prayer was His very life. Everything began and ended in prayer. He prayed before He did things; prayed while He was doing them and prayed for what He had done! He lived to do His Father's will, and that will was received and executed primarily in prayer.

We must all look again at the Lord Jesus and follow His example. We, too, must have a "House of prayer" from which we hardly depart. We must have a "House of prayer" that is "home" for us, from which we go out occasionally to carry out specific duties assigned to us by our loving Father, but to which we return immediately, once the assignment has been accomplished. It is in this way that the believer will be able to fulfil God's call on him to pray without ceasing!

TWELVE YEARS IN THE SCHOOL OF PRAYER

When the Lord Jesus entered the temple at the age of twelve, He was already a Master at the art of praying. He did not automatically know how to pray. He learned it. He spent the first twelve years of His life learning how to do the most important 'must' of His life. He was taught by His heavenly Father. He must have given Himself totally to it.

It is to be expected that the disciple will enrol in God's School of Prayer, spend many years there and from Him learn the art of praying. It is also to be expected that the wise disciple should enrol in the "School of Prayer" of some saint who has been taught of God to pray, and there learn from man how to pray. In that way that saint will supplement what was received in God's School of

Prayer with what is received in Man's School of Prayer and, thereby, make rapid progress.

The problem of our day is that there are very few who want to pay the price of enrolment in God's School of Prayer. In addition to this, the Schools of Prayer of Men of God are hardly existent; the men of prayer are in short supply and even when you find them, there are not many lovers of the Lord who want to stay around them and learn the divine art.

You may be one of those rare figures that are bent on praying. Ask the Lord to enrol you in His School of Prayer. He will do it. Work out your timetable. You will begin in the first class even though you might have believed many years ago. You will grow in the time spent with God in prayer and in the quality of praying. I do hope that the quality of your praying will grow as you grow in the quantity of prayer.

CLASS	TIME SPENT IN PRAYER
one	thirty minutes
two	one hour
three	one hour and thirty minutes
four	two hours
five	two hours and thirty minutes
six	three hours
seven	three hours and thirty minutes
eight	four hours

The time spent in prayer is that of active communion with God hearing His voice and talking back to Him. It is time of intense communion during which the entire being is lost in God. Even if you can occasionally throw words at God for two, three or four hours, you should consider yourself as only in class one if all you know are thirty minutes of sustained communion with God, during which you are not distracted. You may find that you should learn to honestly make progress in the first year as follows :

MONTH	TIME SPENT IN PRAYER IN ONE SITTING
1-2	five minutes
3-4	ten minutes
5-6	fifteen minutes
7-8	twenty minutes
9-10	twenty five minutes
11-12	thirty minutes

You should bear in mind that the primary essence in prayer is communion with God. You may find that there will be times during which you may have to spend thirty minutes in preparation before God in order to be able to have five minutes of communion with Him. As you make progress, you will find that you need less and less time to prepare for communion with Him. This is because as you grow in Him you will begin to increasingly pray without ceasing; so that your special times of praying will only be a continuation of a life of continuous praying. As such, there will be no need for times spent in getting in touch with and "plugging-in" to God; for one has not plugged out.

4

THE HOUSE OF PRAYER

We saw that when the Lord Jesus got to Jerusalem, "He entered the temple and began to drive out those who sold and those who bought in the temple, and he overturned the tables of the money-changers and the seats of those who sold pigeons; and he would not allow anyone to carry anything through the temple. And he taught, and said to them, 'Is it not written, "*My house shall be called a house of prayer for all the nations*"? But you have made it a den of thieves' " (Mark 11:15-17). This was at the end of His ministry. At the beginning of His ministry, He had done a similar thing. The Bible says, "The Passover of the Jews was at hand, and Jesus went up to Jerusalem. In the temple he found those who were selling oxen and sheep and pigeons, and the money-changers at their business. And making a whip of cords, he drove them all, with the sheep and oxen, out of the temple; and he poured out the coins of the money-changers and overturned their tables. And he told those who sold the pigeons, "*Take those things away; you shall not make my Father's house a house of trade*" " (John 2:13-16).

The Lord cleansed the temple of all the religious businesses that were taking place in it. He did not even allow the selling of oxen, sheep and pigeons that were necessary for sacrifices. He knew that His Father's house was a house of prayer and only prayer ought to be allowed there. The cleansing of His Father's house was of such importance to Him that He carried it out twice, once at the beginning of His ministry and a second time at the end of it. It was of such critical importance that He used a whip of cords the only such incident in His entire life on earth.

The believer's spirit is his house of prayer. It is here that the Holy Spirit dwells and receives from the Father and gives to the believer as the Lord Jesus has said, "*He will glorify me; for he will take what is mine and declare it to you*" (John 16:14). The Holy Spirit takes the will of the Father and reveals it to the believer's spirit and takes what is in the believer's spirit and brings it to the Father.

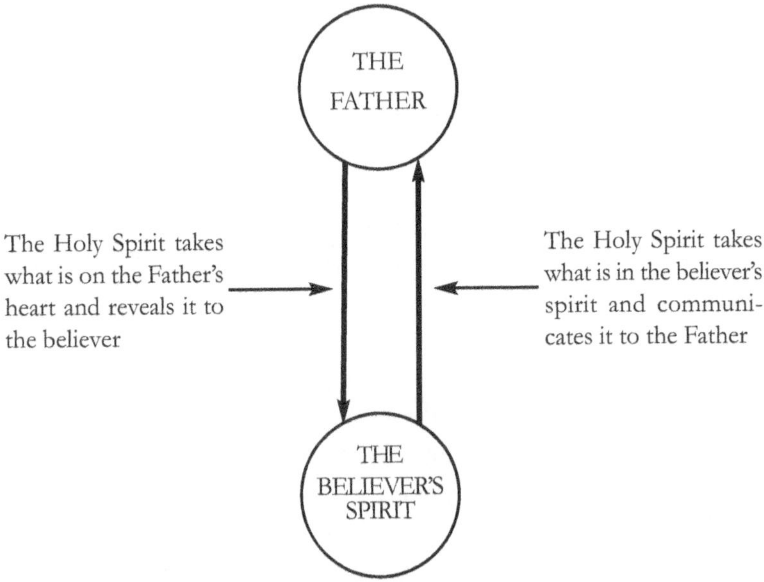

Since the spirit of the believer is the place of contact and communion with the Holy Spirit, and since there is no other way by which the believer can enter into communion with God except through the Holy Spirit, we can say that the spirit of the believer is the place where prayer really takes place; for there the believer receives God's will and prays it back to the Father.

This means that the spirit of the believer must be pure and consecrated. Any sin in a believer's life will severely hinder his prayer life. This does not only apply to the grosser sins like theft, immorality and the like that can be committed in act, but also to those sins that are "sins of the heart." The following are some of the sins of the heart that will hinder or reduce the effectiveness of a man's prayer life, even if there may be no outward acts of these:

1. Pride
2. Vanity
3. Love of the world
4. Love of the things of the world
5. Self-love
6. Self-exaltation
7. Self-justification
8. Self-defence
9. Self-praise
10. A critical spirit
11. A spirit that judges others
12. A spirit that condemns others
13. Every form of falsehood
14. Every form of self-deception
15. Covetousness
16. Envy
17. Jealousy
18. Impure thoughts
19. Wicked thoughts
20. Any other such sins.

The believer who would make progress in the Ministry of Prayer must get rid of all such sins. He must be pure in spirit. He must do this, first of all, by being observant and, consequently, confessing any such sins that are manifested in his life and also by labouring to enter into the sanctified life in which such sins are rare.

Such a believer will not only labour to have a pure spirit, but will also labour to ensure that he does not have an encumbered spirit that is carrying things that though not sinful are useless in helping him to run the race. He will not expose his spirit to the excitement of worldly things, be they legal things, but will seek deliberately to separate himself unto God and protect his spirit from those things that should have no place in it.

The believer is thus to ask about every motive, thought, word or action:

1. Will it hinder my spirit from being receptive?
2. Will it disturb the peace of my spirit?
3. Will it move my spirit from its condition of rest before God?

By the answers to these questions, the believer is to build a wall around his spirit; so as to defend it from invasion by destabilising forces. The Lord said, "Blessed are the pure in heart for they shall see God." We add, "Blessed are the pure in heart for they shall pray effectively."

Make it your aim to keep your house of prayer pure and consecrated! Amen.

5

EIGHTEEN CRUCIAL YEARS

The ministry of the Lord Jesus can be put on scale as below:

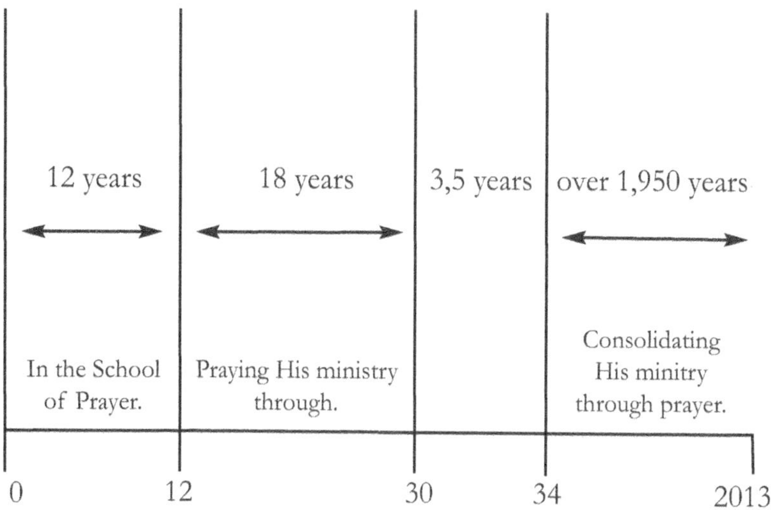

There were the twelve years during which He learnt to pray. At the age of twelve, when He appeared in the temple, His knowledge of God and man was such that the Bible says, "*And all who heard him were amazed at his understanding and his answers*" (Luke 2:47). The Lord was well able to start His ministry then. After all He could have decided to start earlier; so that He would have more time to really invest into it. Why did He have to wait for another eighteen years? There may be other reasons for it, but the main reason was that the Lord Jesus needed to pray His ministry through before God, before He could carry it out before man. He knew that what really took place during the ministry depended on what took place before the ministry in the place of prayer with God and in the place of warfare against the devil. So He carried out His entire ministry five times over before God and against the devil before He appeared in public to face both man and the devil. The Lord was so convinced about this that He put eighteen years into it, leaving a meagre three and a half years for the accomplishment of the outward ministry.

So the Lord spent eighteen years to pray a three-and-a-half-year ministry through. He spent five years in prayer for every year of public ministry that He was to carry out.

We conclude that for anyone who wants to follow in the steps of the Lord Jesus and to exercise the same influence over men, demons and evil spirits, the prerequisite is as follows:

- 5 hours of prayer for every hour of ministry;
- 5 days of prayer for every day of ministry;
- 5 years of prayer for every year of ministry.

If the Lord Jesus Christ; whose communion with God was perfect, who was always full of the Holy Spirit, who had all authority and power in heaven and on earth, needed to pray His ministry through with such intensity and for so many years, then those of us who have relegated prayer to a second place are only labouring to our shame. He said, "*Truly, truly, I say to you, he who believes in me will also do the works that I do; and greater works than these will he do, because I go to the Father. Whatever you ask in my name, I will do it, that the Father may be glorified in the Son; if you ask anything in my name, I will do it*" (John 14:12-14). The Lord's promise that the believer would do the works that He did and do greater works than He did was in a context of the believer asking whatever and asking anything in His name. It becomes obvious that the asking and the receiving would be of the quality and quantity that was manifested in His own life. May we, therefore, not conclude that the believer who prays for five years for every year of ministry would do the works that the Lord did? Might we also not say that the believer who prays more than the Lord prayed, that is, praying ten years for every year of ministry will do greater works than the Lord did? Might we also not say that the poor spiritual condition of the Church today and her very limited impact on the world is owing to too little praying? Is it fair to pray less than the Lord prayed and hope to do the works that He did? Is it not true that the average pastor or evangelist does not know the basic experience of one hour of prayer each day as a minimum?

Many Churches have two hours of service on Sunday and some other meeting for other activities in the week. For a normal Church that has a two-hour worship or evangelistic or teaching ministry on Sunday, honesty would have demanded ten hours of praying in order to prepare those hours of meeting before God and frustrating the devil's purposes for those hours. The question is, How many local assemblies are practising that? Do you know of any? If you find one such, it will be a flourishing assembly; for the people of God cannot follow the example of the Lord in prayer and not see the great things that He promised happen.

The preacher who will pray for ten hours and preach for to hours on Sunday or on any other day will see great things happen. I dare say that it will be absolutely impossible to pray for ten hours every week for a two-hour sermon and not see far-reaching changes. The dull of hearing will begin to hear; the disobedient will begin to obey; the worldly will begin to find the world distasteful; unbelievers will begin to understand the gospel and be saved; a ministry like that of the Lord will become visible again and God will be glorified!

Looking at things this way, it becomes obvious that the people of God can cause the next great move of God to take place. The problem is not that God is not able to do great things or does not want to do them. The problem is that He has bound Himself to move in proportion to the prayers of His people. Because His people are praying so little, He can do very little. If they prayed more, He would do more. If they gave themselves to prayer, He would give Himself to causing great and mighty works to be done in their midst!

Lest anyone should become discouraged because he is alone, we say that for an individual who prays ten hours a week for the lost and spends two hours a week witnessing to them, the power of God will so move in his life and ministry that many will be converted who will abide in the Lord.

When the apostle Peter was locked up, the Bible says, "*So Peter was kept in prison; but earnest prayer for him was made to God by the church*" (Acts 12:5). These earnest prayers were heard and God did a great act. An angel was sent to Peter and he was released from prison. Had the Church not prayed and kept praying, things would have been different. In fact, the Church did not only pray earnestly. The Church prayed without ceasing. The Church prayed from the moment when Peter was arrested to the time when he was released; for he found them still praying!

LONG YEARS OF PRAYER?

We have seen that the Lord prayed for eighteen years for a ministry that was to last only three and a half years. Why was it necessary that He spend so much time in prayer? As we shall see, He spent nights in prayer and has been praying for over one thousand five hundred years in order to consolidate the work that He accomplished in three and a half years. Why must so much time be invested in prayer before God acts?

The truth is that I do not know why God would not do a thing simply because it had been asked once. All I know is that God is not only interested that His will be prayed back to Him for execution. He is anxious and insists that His will be prayed through also quantitatively. It would seem that there is a certain "volume" of praying that must be attained before God would do some things. It would seem that that volume of prayer cannot be arrived at in one time of asking. It would seem that God is prepared to wait and must wait for the believer to bring in the needed volume of prayer; so that He can act. The one who then prays once when he ought to pray a thousand times and the one who prays for one month instead of continuing to pray for eighteen years, will not have answers to those prayers that need eighteen years. He may start very well, but if he would not put in the needed minutes, hours, days or years in prayers, he will be compelled to go away unrewarded. God has ordained it to be that and it is so!

GROUP PRAYING TO MEET PRAYER REQUIREMENTS

This book is going to take 200-250 writing hours to complete. I have already spent many years thinking through the message and trying to work out the practical implications for my life and ministry. If I want to be honest, I should spend 250 X 5 = 1,250 hours in prayer for the book before I can write it. If I were to pray for 5 hours a day, that will take me 250 days to pray the book through before it is written. This might mean that the book will not be written for many years. What I have done has been to share the burden with my prayer partners in the writing ministry whom I call "praying authors." So I am the "writing author" and they the "praying authors." This means that I spend time in prayer that is long enough for me to have an inward flow and then I can write and only return to praying when the inward flow begins to dwindle. Each "praying author" is committed to praying for a certain number of hours for the book and does pray so that by the time the book is finished at least 1,250 prayer hours will have been invested into it.

I am applying the same principle to other aspects of our ministry. For example, I will be going out on a journey that will take me to seven countries to preach the gospel and carry out chemical research. I will be away for 40 days. I do not know when I shall be ministering and when I shall not.

I have, therefore, decided to consider every hour of the forty days as ministry time which is 40 x 24 = 480 hours. In order that there should be 5 hours of praying for each hour of ministry, I need 480 X 5 = 2,400 praying hours. I have made an appeal to my prayer partners and they are sending in their sacrificial contribution of prayer hours. My prayer to God is that the required prayer hours be met, for unless they are met, the trip will be without mandate. I now consider it easier to set out on a journey or to start a special project with insufficient funds than to set out without the necessary praying.

I have to confess that I have only just seen this matter of five-fold praying for each hour of ministry. If I had practised it in the past, things would have been different.

The rationale behind this is that, since God seems to need a certain volume of praying from His children before He can do certain things, He will only act if that volume is provided for by an individual, or collectively by people whose praying is acceptable to Him! This must be the reason why the apostle Paul, who was given to much praying, pleaded with the saints to pray for him. For example, he wrote to the Colossians as follows: "*Continue steadfastly in prayer, being watchful in it with thanksgiving; and pray for us also, that God may open to us a door for the word, to declare the mystery of Christ, on account of which I am in prison, that I may make it clear; as I ought o speak*" (Colossians 4:2-4). To the Ephesians he wrote: "*Pray at all times in the Spirit, with all prayer and supplication. To that end keep alert with all perseverance, making supplication for all the saints, and also for me, that utterance may be given me in opening my mouth boldly to proclaim the mystery of the gospel, for which I am an ambassador in chains; that I may declare it boldly, as I ought to speak*" (Ephesians

6:18-20). He prayed as if all depended on his praying and he pleaded for the saints to pray for him as if all depended on their praying. The combined effect of his praying and their praying was a very fruitful and abundant ministry. The same type of ministry will be the lot of all who are as consecrated as he was, as prayerful as he was, and as prayed for by the same number of consecrated believers, for the same duration that he was prayed for.

COMMITMENTS TO PRAY

There are many people who seek financial co-workers for the ministries to which they feel called by God; these co-workers are expected to commit themselves to give a certain number of dollars each month, and many of them do give faithfully. However, there are few who demand specific commitments to prayer in terms that are measurable like minutes, hours, days, weeks or months. The minister then ought to sum up the commitments to pray, and on that basis know something of the strength of his ministry. He ought to plan future ministry on the availability of prayer and he ought to refuse to move in a new direction, even if funds were available but adequate prayer commitments lacking. The availability of prayer partners and the volume of praying ought to be more indicative of God's permission to move ahead than the availability of funds. The reason is obvious one rich man can with one generous check provide the financial needs of a work for one month or even one year, whereas there are no individuals who can in one minute meet the prayer needs of a work for a month!

WHAT DOES THIS SAY TO YOU?

It ought to say two things: First of all, that work that is not prayed through adequately several times over is actually only an activity of the flesh. It will bring no reward at the Judgment Seat of the praying Christ. It should be stopped at once and things done

God's way prayer and prayer and prayer before the activity. Secondly, you should have a clear strategy for praying for everything you intend to do well ahead of time. Projects that are to be carried out in ten years should begin to be soaked in prayer now. It is not enough to pray alone; recruit prayer partners and organise them properly into a prayer force. Let each commit himself to pray for some time, and let the commitment be checked to ensure that it is not mere words. Let it be settled with God that unless a certain volume of prayer was reached (measured perhaps in "prayer hours") the project should not be allowed to begin. This commitment, strictly followed, will impose the discipline needed in prayer and a new day will dawn on the man of God and his work for God.

Finally, set out your own prayer programme that provides for ten hours of praying for your two hours of ministry, either as a preacher, teacher, evangelist, Sunday School teacher, counsellor and so on. Deliberately refuse any invitation to do any work for which the right price has not been paid in prayer. Amen.

6

BAPTIZED AND PRAYING

"Now when all the people were baptized, and when Jesus had also been baptized and was praying, the heaven was opened, and the Holy Spirit descended upon him in bodily form, as a dove, and a voice came from heaven, Thou art my beloved Son; with thee I am well pleased" (Luke 3:21-22).

As we have seen, the Lord Jesus invested eighteen years in praying through His ministry before He started it in public. He knew that He would have to be baptized in the Jordan. He new that He would have to have the Spirit come upon Him to empower Him in a special way at the very beginning of His public ministry. Knowing these things and having eighteen years to pray them through, He must have prayed and prayed every detail through and through. We might even say that there was no aspect of it which was not adequately prayed through.

So, finally, that day came and the Saviour of the world was there at the Jordan. The people were baptized. As each person was baptized, he would come up out of the water and go away rejoicing and then it would be the turn of the next. Each was baptized and each followed his baptism by either going away or by standing by to watch the others receive theirs at the hand of John the Baptist.

Then came the turn of the Lord Jesus to be baptized. He entered the Jordan and was baptized. Immediately He was baptized, unlike the others, He did not go away or stand by to watch the others receive their baptism. HIS BAPTISM WAS IMMEDIATELY FOL-

LOWED BY A PERSONAL PRAYER MEETING OF GREAT INTENSITY ON THE BANKS OF THE JORDAN.

As He was praying, heaven was opened and the Holy Spirit descended upon Him in bodily form, as a dove, and a voice came from heaven.

The following happened as Jesus was praying:

1. The heaven was opened.
2. The Holy Spirit descended.
3. The Holy Spirit landed on Him.
4. A voice came from heaven.

These things happened partly because Jesus was the Son of God. They also happened partly because He followed His baptism with praying. We can say that He came out of the water of baptism and began to pray. He prayed until the Holy Spirit came down upon Him. Although He was the Son of God and deserved to have the Holy Spirit come down upon Him, the Holy Spirit would most probably not have come down upon Him had He come out of the water of baptism and not prayed. HE PRAYED DOWN THE HOLY SPIRIT UPON HIMSELF.

TAKING GOD FOR GRANTED?

The Lord Jesus knew that the Father had ordained that the Holy Spirit should descend upon Him as a dove. He had prayed this long before the event and settled it before God. The Father had told John the Baptist, "*He on whom you see the Spirit descend and remain, this is he who baptizes with the Holy Spirit*" (John 1:33). So, from God's point of view everything was set for the Holy Spirit to descend on the Lord Jesus.

How did Jesus react, knowing that the Father had ordained this and He had prayed it through? Two pathways were opened to Him. One was to say, "God has ordained this very thing, told John about it and, in addition, I have put in many years praying it through. I need not bother now for it must come to pass." Had He chosen that pathway, He would have been shocked, for He would have waited in vain for the Holy Spirit to descend upon Him. The second pathway was to say, "The Father has ordained that the Holy Spirit should come upon me. He has told John about it and I did put in years of intense labour in prayer about it. Now the event is about to happen. I must exert Myself in utter pleading with My Father so that it should indeed be as He purposed. I must pray; for if it does not happen, my Father's word to John will not come to pass and He would be seen to be a liar. I must pray, lest the Holy Spirit should not come upon Me and the many years of praying be wasted. I must pray because I desperately need the Holy Spirit to descend upon Me." He chose the second pathway and prayed and, as He was praying, heaven was opened and the Holy Spirit came upon Him!

The problem with too many believers is that they fail to enter into the practical experience of the promises of God because they do not pray. They say to themselves: "God has promised this and that thing in the Word and, therefore, it is mine because it has been promised." Yes, the truth is that it is available according to the promise of God, but only those who lay hold of the promises of God through prayer will enter into their inheritance. To be promised an inheritance is one thing. To enter into the promised inheritance is quite another!

The apostle, in writing to the Corinthians, put it this way: "*I want you to know, brethren that our fathers were all under the cloud, and all passed through the sea, and all were baptised into Moses in the cloud and in the sea, and all ate the same supernatural food and all drank the same supernatural drink. For they drank from the supernatural Rock which followed them, and the Rock was Christ. Nevertheless with most of them God was not pleased; for they were overthrown in the wilderness*" (1 Corinthians 10:1-5). It could also be said of the Church in our day that the Lord has done so much for her and made so many promises to bless her, but for most of them the promises have been made of no avail by her prayerlessness. ANYONE WHO EXPECTS ANY PROMISE OF GOD TO BE FULFILLED IN HIS LIFE OR IN THE LIFE OF THE CHURCH WITHOUT SUSTAINED CO-OPERATION IN PRAYER, IS MISTAKEN. ANYONE WHO THINKS THAT BECAUSE HE PRAYED IN THE PAST, HE CAN RELAX AT THE MOMENT AND YET REAP THE FULL FRUIT OF GOD'S CURRENT MOVE, IS SELF-DECEIVED.

The one who knows God and the laws of prayer will pray intensely before an event and continue to pray intensely at the moment of realization. He will pray long before the event with utter intensity, labouring as if there will be no other opportunity to pray (and there may be no other). At the moment of realization or fulfilment, he must pray with such utter intensity as if his prayer in the past was of no consequence and everything depended upon what he is doing now in prayer. This is the way to follow the example of the Lord. He prayed in the past and He kept praying in the present.

Someone may ask, "Is it not unbelief to keep praying when an answer has been promised?" To this we say that a promise of an answer is a great invitation to co-operate with God for its realization. This co-operation is largely through prayer. God has never blamed anyone for asking without ceasing. The promise of God to do something needs to be prayed through until it is realized because there are other sides to the issue. First of all, prayer strengthens the character and faith of the one who prays and thus prepares him to better handle the blessings when they come. Secondly, God has an enemy who is bent on thwarting His purposes. That enemy is the devil. Immediately God makes a promise, His enemy goes to work to see how best to prevent that promise from being fulfilled. It is when the praying believer co-operates with God in unceasing prayer that the plans of the enemy to destroy are put to naught and the original purpose of God is fulfilled. Do we take for granted that a baby will be born in good health simply because there is a pregnancy? Of course not! Many things can go wrong and lead to a miscarriage or to a stillbirth or, worse, to a deformed baby. The wise person does everything to protect the pregnancy.

God's promises are like pregnancies. Whether or not a healthy child will be born does not only depend on the praying that led to the pregnancy, but even more so on the praying that ensures that the baby grows normally and is protected from disease. Even a baby who has grown healthy for nine months in the womb might yet die at delivery. Such a death would be most expensive because of all that would have been put in to bring the pregnancy that far. Consequently, the greatest care and the best expertise is required at the stage of delivery. The Lord Jesus knew all this and that is why as He came out of the Jordan He engaged Himself in violent praying that continued until the Holy Spirit had descended and remained on Him as His Father had spoken. We, too, must follow suit and labour in prayer until faith gives way to sight.

PRAYING AND THE DESCENT OF THE HOLY SPIRIT

We have seen that the Holy Spirit descended on a praying Christ. We also know that the Holy Spirit descended upon the praying 120 in the upper room; for the Bible says, "*All these with one accord devoted themselves to prayer, together with the women and Mary the mother of Jesus, and with his brothers... When the day of Pentecost had fully come, they were all together in one place. And suddenly a sound came from heaven like the rush of a mighty wind, and it filled all the house where they were sitting. And there appeared to them tongues as of fire, distributed and resting on each one of them. And they were all filled with the Holy Spirit and began to speak in other tongues, as the Spirit gave them utterance*" (Acts 1:14; 2:1-4). So, the Holy Spirit came upon this group of disciples who had devoted themselves to prayer!

The Bible again says, "*And when they had prayed, the place in which they were gathered together was shaken; and they were all filled with the Holy Spirit and spoken the word of God with boldness*" (Acts 4:31). It was to praying Saul that Ananias was sent that he might receive his sight and be filled with the Holy Spirit (Acts 9:11, 17).

The Lord Jesus did not only demonstrate the relationship between prayer and the descent of the Holy Spirit by what happened in His own life. He also taught it. He said, "If you then, who are evil, know how to give good gifts to your children, how much more will the heavenly Father give the Holy Spirit to those who ask him!" Yes, the Father will give the Holy Spirit for the first time to those who ask Him. He will pour the Holy Spirit a second time upon the one who asks Him. He will continue to cause the Holy Spirit to descend in fuller measure on those of His children who pay a continuous price of being devoted in asking him!

7

LORD, OPEN THE HEAVENS!

As we have seen, as the Lord Jesus came out of the Jordan and was praying, heaven was opened! Heaven was closed until He prayed. When heaven was opened, the Holy Spirit descended and the voice of the Father was heard.

The prophet Isaiah cried, "O that thou wouldst rend the heavens and come down, that the mountains might quake at thy presence as when fire kindles brushwood and the fire causes water to boil to make thy name known to thy adversaries, and that the nations might tremble at thy presence!" (Isaiah 64:1-2).

The Psalmist cried, "Bow thy heavens, O Lord, and come down! Tough the mountains that they smoke! Flash forth the lightning and scatter them, send out thy arrows and rout them! Stretch forth thy hand from on high, rescue me and deliver me from the many waters, from the hand of aliens, whose mouths speak lies, and whose right hand is a right hand of falsehood" (Psalm 144:5-8).

There is a sense in which the heavens remain sealed until the person of prayer prays and God, in answer to prayer, rends the heavens and comes down or pours out blessings on His people and destroys the enemies of His people.

There were the prayers of the Lord Jesus that rent the heavens and caused the Holy Spirit to descend upon Him. God was ready to send the Holy Spirit, but how could He come through the sealed heavens? When the prayers of Jesus went up they broke the barrier, rent the heavens and the obstacle was removed and down came the Holy Spirit upon Him. He was the first beneficiary of the descent of the Holy Spirit that followed the rending of the heavens.

An individual believer could cause the heavens; to be rent so that the power of the Lord should descend upon him. You and I are called to that.

An individual believer could cause the heavens to be rent so that the power of the Lord should descend and put to naught the power of Satan that is arrayed against him. You and I are called to rend the heavens so that the power of that Lord might descend and put to naught the spirits of lust, greed, covetousness and all the like that are arrayed against the saints today.

An individual believer can rend the heavens; so that the Lord should descend and bless his :

- Assembly,
- Ministry
- Town,
- Nation,
- Continent, and
- Planet.

There is no limit to the blessings that would be received if the heavens were opened by a believer.

An individual believer can also rend the heavens; so that the Lord should descend and put to naught the power of Satan working in his family, local assembly, city, nation, continent or planet. In this way, a single believer can wield limitless power and authority that is needed for the overthrow of the kingdom of the evil one.

Although individuals can rend the heavens through their prayers and, as a consequence bring much blessing on the people of God, as well as much harm against the purposes of the evil one, the Lord's ultimate purpose is that the Church should carry out that task of rending the heavens for her good and for the destruction of the Enemy. There is another issue involved. It is more difficult for one consecrated believer to rend the heavens than for a fellowship of consecrated believers to do so. God, while respecting and blessing individual activity, has His eyes turned to the Church as a body and not just to individuals. It is for this reason that He said in His Word, "*And you shall chase your enemies, and they shall fall before you by the sword. Five of you shall chase a hundred and a hundred of you shall chase ten thousand; and your enemies shall fall before you by the sword*" (Leviticus 26:7-8). When five people confront the Enemy and chase a hundred of them, each person is chasing twenty, whereas, when a hundred confront the enemy and chase ten thousand of them, each is chasing one hundred. The Lord intends that the corporate prayer life of the Church should result in the five-fold increase in spiritual accomplishment.

There may be situations under which one consecrated believer may pray and pray in vain without the needed power for basic breakthrough. Take, for example, a nation that has hardened itself consistently against the Lord and has specialized in the sins that are a special abomination to the Lord like witchcraft, sorcery and the like. Such a nation, having received light in the past and turned away from that light and stood against God by specialising in these sins for, maybe, centuries, will have the heavens specially sealed against her, and it may not be possible for one consecrated believer to raise the prayer force that will rend the heavens and cause the Holy Spirit to fall upon the people of that land, to soften their hearts towards God.

We recommend that there be prayer battles that are best entered into in a corporate way. If a believer can raise other believers to join in the prayer battle but refuses to do so because of pride or because of an individualistic or party spirit, he will not see the full victory of the Lord. However, if there is no one who can be recruited to join in the prayer battle, there being only one believer who will fight wholeheartedly for the Lord, the Lord is able to strengthen that one so that, alone, he is able to do great exploits for the Lord. In fact, he may even be so enabled that alone he will accomplish what five warriors could not accomplish. The Lord said to the Israelites, "*One man of you puts to flight a thousand, since it is the Lord your God who fights for you, as he promised you*" (Joshua 23:10).

MAN RENDING THE HEAVENS

There are situations in which a man should in prayer come directly against the heavens that are sealed and rend them; so that the blessings of the Lord may fall upon himself or upon others who are in need. If the Lord has made a promise, then it is only fair to address the heavens that have remained sealed and command them to open. In such cases, we talk directly to the obstacle and command it to be gone. It could be a satanic force that continues to seal a heaven that the Lord has already opened. That force is to be commanded to let go and that with insistence until it has let go and the victory is won.

It should be realized that man rending the heavens is no child's play. It may take consecrated believers hours, days, weeks and perhaps years of constant knocking for there to be release. The force that will not yield to one, ten, one hundred, one thousand or one million prayer blows may begin to weaken at the knock of one billion, ten billion, one hundred billion or one trillion blows over an extended period. What the warrior must realize is that victory is inevitable and that it will come if he presses hard enough for long enough. You can rend the heavens that remain sealed over a certain individual, family, city, nation, continent or planet. You can rend the heavens that remain sealed; so that the power of the Lord should release some people from a certain ignorance. You can rend the heavens over a nation or tribe; so that God should move there in a special way and cause the people to turn to the Lord. You can do that. Do it. Do not just pray in a general way. Let the Lord lead you to a particular tribe or people and there consecrate your blows to rend the heavens. One day the sealed heavens will be broken and the blessing will flow. On that day more people may be saved in one day than at the moment in ten years. It will be the Lord's special day and He wants you to help and bring it to pass. Do something about it!

GOD RENDING THE HEAVENS

God is able to rend the heavens any time He wants to, so that there should be untold and limitless blessings on the sons of men and on His children. However, by sovereign choice, He has decided not to do so until His children ask Him to. Sometimes He will only do it if they insist that He should do it. At other times and in some specific situations, He has ordained that He will not do it until a certain number of His children ask Him and continue to ask Him over a sustained period of asking. God just delights in having His children participate, through prayer, in the ruling of the universe. Because that is the way He has chosen that things should be done, we consequently put aside our rationalization and obey Him. If He demands that one consecrated believer should ask Him once so that the heavens be opened, then that is what is to be done. If, on the other hand, He wants one consecrated believer to ask night and day for one decade, let that be so. If, on the other hand, the situation is such that it needs one hundred consecrated believers praying night and day for ten years before the heavens open, then let the price be paid and He will act. The full price must be paid in asking Him to open the heavens before one can expect the heavens to be fully open.

The intercessor will then pray, pleading that the Lord should open the heavens. He will keep at it until it is done. It may not be long before it is done. He may, on the other hand, find that it is not just a matter of asking God to open the heavens, but that there is real resistance and the Lord will have to rend the heavens. He then knows that that is a situation for warfare and he might have to exert himself and others in sustained conflict.

PARTIAL OR FULL RENDING OF THE HEAVENS

It is possible to rend the heavens in full measure and have the full measure of what God has in store for you, for a family, city, nation or continent or it is possible to rend heaven only partially and have only a portion of the blessings that the Lord intended for you to have or to bring to your family, city, nation or continent.

The Word of the Lord says, "*Ask rain from the Lord in the season of the spring rain, from the Lord who makes the storm clouds, who gives men showers of rain, to everyone the vegetation in the field*" (Zechariah 10:1). The Word continues to say, "*And if you will obey my commandments which I command you this day, to love the Lord your God, and to serve him with all your heart and with all your soul, he will give the rain for your land in its season, the early rain and the later rain, that you may gather in your grain and your wine and your oil*" (Deuteronomy 11:13-14). And, "*Be glad, O sons of Zion, and rejoice in the Lord, your God; for he has given the early rain for your vindication, he has poured down for you abundant rain, the early and the latter rain, as before*" (Joel 2:23).

So there are two types of rains the early and the latter rain. Those who press on with the Lord and refuse to be distracted off the Lord by current blessings, will receive the current blessings and the blessings yet to come.

It is a matter for much regret that when a man or a people have just begun to rend the heavens or they have asked and God has just begun to rend the heavens; so that the first drops of rain begin to fall, most have stopped the praying, turned their eyes from the Lord and focussed them on the blessing and, as a result, caused the blessing to stop short of what God had in mind. They then have a limited blessing which may later on be a burden.

I have often thought about the leftovers of the revivals of the past systems, organizations, denominations, buildings and a religious phraseology that is difficult to change, and wondered if in some cases this was not the only abiding fruit of the revival! God was not allowed to accomplish His total purpose. The Enemy succeeded in having people who ought to make the Lord the goal, make the revival the goal. They tried to preserve the atmosphere and the outward forms that accompanied the revival, even when God had stopped to move.

To avoid such folly in the coming move of God, we must love the Lord profoundly and be satisfied in Him. We must pray for the early rain of His blessings and insist that He should move in an unparalleled way. We must keep insisting until He begins to move. When He has begun to move, we must enter into storming heaven in a most desperate, insistent and persistent way; so that He should continue to move and so that the greater and more permanent blessings which He normally reserves for later days be brought down. We must continue to look to Him, move with Him and thank Him for that which we have already received, while insisting in prayer that the best is yet to come. And it will come!

DO NOT GIVE UP JUST BEORE BREAKING THROUGH

My beloved father told me a story on the need to persevere. He said that an animal was caught in a trap. Throughout the night it laboured to get free. The trap began to eat into its flesh and soon the wound got deeper and deeper in the foot where the animal was caught. All this while, the animal bore the pain silently. Somewhere near four o'clock in the morning, it gave up hope and began to cry aloud. The man who had set the trap heard the cry and rushed to where the trap was and killed the animal. On examining it at home, he found that the animal's foot was almost completely cut through by the trap and only a few threads of tendon were left. He calculated that if he had got there a few minutes later, he would only have found a small piece of the animal's foot in the trap, whereas the animal would have been gone. That animal died because it did not press on to the end. It was impatient.

Many believers are like that. They give up just on the brink of success. Have you stormed heaven on your behalf or on the behalf of your family, ministry, city or nation for hours, weeks, years and not yet seen the heavens open? Do not give up. You may be on the brink of success. It may be that one more hour, day, week, month or year of praying will cause the final breakthrough to come and then everything will be different. Hold on! Do not give up. There may be no sign on the horizon that the needed blessings are about to come. Do not be put off by that. The changes in the spiritual horizon may be taking place slowly in the hearts of men while the exterior remains apparently untouched. God often works from the inside to the outside. The work may be at a mature state in the inside and soon the outward shell will crack in one go and then there will be release. So press on! Hold on! Exert yourself with that last bit of energy in prayer. Summon other people to pray. Hold that additional all-night prayer meeting. Go on! Press on! Victory will soon be yours, and then the Lord's name will be glorified and you edified.

Draw courage from the experience of another warrior with the heavens. The Bible says, "And Elijah said to Ahab, 'Go up, eat and drink; for there is a sound of the rushing of rain.' So Ahab went up to eat and to drink. And Elijah went up to the top of Carmel; and he bowed himself down upon the earth, and put his face between his knees. And he said to his servant, 'Go up now, look toward the sea.' And he went up and looked, and said, 'There is nothing.' And he said, 'Go again seven times.' And at the seventh time he said, 'Behold, a little cloud like a man's hand is rising out of the sea.' And he said, 'Go up, say to Ahab, "*Prepare your chariot and go down, lest the rain stop you.*" ' And in a little while the heavens grew black with clouds and wind, and there was a great rain" (1 Kings 18:41-45).

Be like Elijah. Continue in prayer as he continued in the posture of a woman in labour. Put in everything like a woman who must have her baby delivered. There was probably no apparent response for your six initial hours, days, months or years of praying. However, the seventh is just about to dawn on you and all will then come to completion and to execution. The little cloud like a man's hand will soon appear and a little while from then there will not only be rain. There will be a great rain. Praise the Lord!

8

GOD BEFORE MAN

"*That evening, at sundown, they brought to him all who were sick or possessed with demons. And the whole city was gathered together about the door. And he healed many who were sick with various diseases, and cast out many demons; and he would not permit the demons to speak, because they knew him.*

And in the morning, a great while before day, he rose and went out to a lonely place and there he prayed. And Simon and those who were with him pursued him, and they found him and said to him, 'Everyone is searching for you.' And he said to them, 'Let us go on to the next towns that I may preach there also; for that is why I came out.' And he went throughout all Galilee, preaching in their synagogues and casting out demons" (Mark 1:32-39).

The evening before, the Lord had healed many who were sick with various diseases and cast out many demons; he could have gone to bed drunk with His manifest power and glory. He could have said, 'Now that it is this way, I must see what more miracles will be performed the next day for the crowds, in order to sustain their interest in Me. I must wake up early and be at the place where the crowd is, so that their interest in Me does not wane and so that no one steals My glory and My honour.

However, the Lord did not do that. He was indifferent to the praises of men. Crowds did not mean anything to Him outside the fact that they needed to have their needs met by Him, and He was willing to be used that way.

There was, however, something that meant everything to the

Lord Jesus. That thing was His relationship with His heavenly Father.

COSTLY FELLOWSHIP

We read that the Lord Jesus, in the morning, a great while before day, went out to a lonely place and there He prayed. He wanted special prayer fellowship with His Father and He paid the price for it. He chose the morning hours when He was most fresh. He decided that He would ensure that there was no disturbance. If He just stayed where He spent the night, He would run the risk of having His prayer fellowship with God interfered with. He thus put a distance between Himself and those who might want Him to minister to them, so that His time with God might be in undisturbed silence. Roads were not what they are today. It was no comfort to withdraw to a lonely place.

He chose the time, a great while before day. Those were the times when most people enjoyed sleep. The best sleep is the early morning sleep; that is between 4.00 and 6.00 o'clock. The Lord decided to deprive Himself of the best hours of sleep; so that He might talk to His Father. Yes, He woke up not just in the morning, not just before day, not just a while before day, but a great while before day. He chose to start a great while before day, so that He might have enough time to pray before it was day. He knew that people would start to seek Him when it was day but that there was every chance that He could commune with His Father before anyone came with the needs of man.

So He maintained this routine of waking up a great while before day, every day of His life, and that made all the difference in His relationship with His Father and man. It left a great impact on His ministry.

GOD BEFORE MAN

In withdrawing to pray a great while before day the Lord Jesus was placing things in the right order. He decided not to see the face of man before He had seen the face of His Father. He decided not to talk to man about God before He had talked to God about man. He decided not to deal with the opinions of men about God but to impose the will of God for man upon man. He decided that He would seek God, know what He wanted and then come amongst men and execute what God wanted. He decided to receive the blueprint of each day from the Lord and, as such, do everything for the purpose and by the method that His Father wanted.

In those early Morning Prayer sessions, the Lord Jesus waited on His Father and heard Him. He was shown what the Father was doing in heaven, so that He might act accordingly on earth. He could consequently say, "*Truly, truly, I say to you, the Son can do nothing of his own accord, but only what he sees the Father doing, for whatever he does, that the Son does likewise. For the Father loves the Son, and shows him all that he himself is doing; and greater works than these will he show him, that you may marvel*" (John 5:19-20).

Do you notice that the Lord Jesus was speaking in the present tense? For example He said, "He sees what the Father is doing." "The Father shows the Son." So it was not just a matter of what was seen while the Son was in heaven but what was daily communicated to Him.

I think of it with a sense of great joy and great expectancy, what went on between the Lord Jesus and His blessed Father. They had unceasing communion with each other but there was this period set apart each day during which the Son withdrew. During those times the Son forgot everything else and everyone else and was preoccupied, lost, enraptured by His Father. It was at the beginning of everyday and it was the beginning of everything for the day. He received renewed strength from His Father. He received renewed encouragement and He received instructions about the day that was before Him. Possibly the Father told Him all that He would encounter in the day. He probably told Him, "They will bring You a blind man. This is what You shall do to restore his sight. You will be confronted with a man possessed with a deaf and dumb demon. You shall deliver him by doing this and that. Someone is going to come to tempt You by asking You the following question. This is how You are to answer that one..." Receiving the Father's will with such clarity and in such detail, He came into the day with authority and confidence. He faced the day with knowledge of what would come to pass and what was the Father's will (which is what He had to do) in each case. How could He have failed? How could He miss the Father's will? How could He have lacked the strength and the courage that was needed? He was a total Success.

The nature of the intimacy and the type of things that were discussed meant that privacy was of great importance. It is for that reason that He withdrew to a lonely place and there prayed. He withdrew to a lonely place and there sorted out everything with God. It was a wonderful time. Often He was so lost in God that He did not know how fast time had gone. For example, in the incident that we have just looked at, He was lost in His fellowship with His Father until Peter intruded into the holy privacy. It was not a burden to Him. He did not gasp for speech waiting for time to roll by. Every minute was a blessed time and He laboured to ensure that before anyone came to interfere, He would have had as much of His Father as time permitted and would have sorted out as many things with His Father as would allow for a successful day. He knew He would contact the Father during the day, but He also knew that there would be a difference between those contacts when people were pressing on Him from every direction and this special time when He was alone with His Father. That is why He maintained that routine of communion with His Father everyday, a great while before day, throughout His earthly ministry. Peter knew His habit and when the people sought Him and He was not available, Peter knew that He had certainly withdrawn to a lonely place as usual, and so he went there and behold, He was there!

THE NEEDS OF HIS DISCIPLES TODAY

The Lord Jesus hungered for His Father and so withdrew everyday to meet Him, enjoy Him and hear Him, as well as talk to Him. He did it as the first thing the initial activity of each day. It was as if all else would collapse if He did not meet God on any morning.

It is to be expected that the disciples of today will develop the same intimacy and desire for their heavenly Father, so that what was true of the begotten Son should also be true of the adopted sons. Cries like those of the Psalmist: "*O God, thou art my God, I seek thee, my soul thirsts for thee; my flesh faints for thee, as in a dry and weary land where no water is. So I have looked upon thee in the sanctuary, beholding thy power and glory. Because thy steadfast love is better than life, my lips will praise thee. So I will bless thee as long as I live; I will lift up my hands and call on thy name*" (Psalm 63:1-4) are rare. However, such cries that include the confession "*As a hart longs for flowing streams, so longs my soul for thee, O God. My soul thirsts for God, for the living God. When shall I come and behold the face of God?*" (Psalm 42:1-2) ought to be the normal cries of the disciple of today. Unfortunately, that which ought to be normal and available in all who are His, has become something so rare that when one finds a person hungry for God, one has found one who is very much the exception.

The question must arise as to why the Lord Jesus loved His Father so much and the disciples of today love Him so little. The question must also be asked why the Lord found the time of prayer-fellowship with His Father each morning so indispensable that He maintained it regularly, whereas many of His disciples of today do not seem to bother about prayer or at least they do not treat it as a priority.

The answer lies in the fact that whereas the Father was the sole object of the supreme love of the Lord Jesus' heart, soul and body, He is not that to the disciples of today. He was in love with the Father. The disciples of today are in love with themselves, with the things of the world and with the people of the world. The clear teaching of Scripture which says, "*Do not love the world or the things in the world. If anyone loves the world, love for the Father is not in him. For all that is in the world, the lust of the flesh and the lust of the eyes and the pride of life, is not of the Father but of the world. And the world passes away, and the lust of it; but he who does the will of God abides for ever*" (1 John 2:15-17) has not been heeded by the disciples of today. Because many believers did not take the warning not to love the world or the things that are in the world seriously, they went ahead and loved the world and the things in it, and in the process of it, they found that no love for the Father was left in their hearts. The love of the world and the things in the world had slowly but steadily consumed the passion of their hearts, so that there was nothing to pour on the Lord. The world and the things of the world having made inroads and captivated the hearts of the believers, made those hearts dull towards God. Such dull hearts do not love Him enough to sacrifice the goddess sleep in order to go out to a lonely place at 4.00 am in search of Him.

The hearts of too many believers are given in love to too many people or too deeply to one person. There was no one else occupying a special place in the heart of the Lord Jesus and, therefore, He had all of His heart to pour out to His Father. Today the saints are too intimately caught up with too many people and too many lovers. Their hearts are divided. Few are those who can say to the Lord, "*Whom have I in heaven but thee? And there is nothing upon earth that I desire besides thee*" (Psalm 73:25).

My beloved reader, can you truly say the following:

"Lord, there is nothing that I desire upon earth besides Thee"?

"Lord, there is no one else that I desire upon earth besides Thee"?

If you can say it, blessed are you. Your heart is free from things and from people. You can pour it out to the Lord. You can grow in the love of Him. If there is something or someone that you desire besides the Lord or in addition to Him, then you have limited yourself. You cannot love Him supremely until He is your only love. If you are going to make progress in desiring and loving Him, you must also make progress in getting all things and all people away from His throne which is your heart.

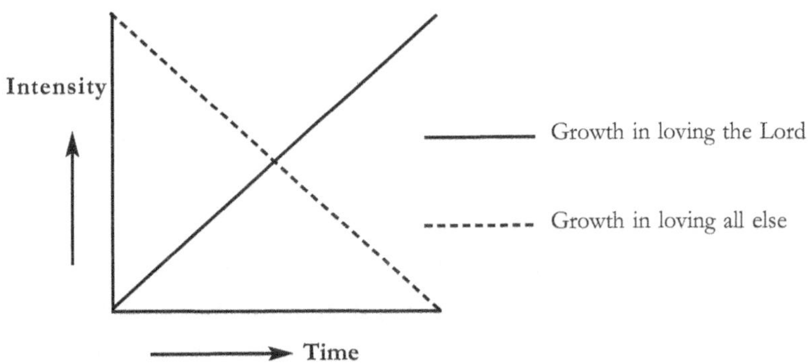

The heart that steadily grows in the love of the Lord will also grow in being dispossessed of people and things. As the place occupied by things and people is increasingly given over the Lord, the heart grows both in the desire and the love of the Lord.

There is a fundamental law of the heart that the children of God need to know. It is that the heart has limited volume. That volume must be occupied. The normal heart is filled with all else but the Lord. At conversion, the Lord enters the heart and begins to occupy the heart to the extent to which the other occupants are removed from it. Where any occupant is allowed to stay, there the Lord must stay off. The heart is made glad and draws close to that which occupies it. If it is the Lord, then that one will desire the Lord intensely. If it is other things, then those things will pull the person towards them. To allow other things in the heart and hope to grow in the Lord, is self-deception.

WHAT HAS THIS GOT TO DO WITH PRAYER?

The question may be raised by some as to what this matter of what possesses the heart has to do with prayer. The thing is this: Prayer is union with the Lord. It is deepest communion with Him. It is more than asking and receiving. It is fusion with Him. The person, whose heart is fused to the things and people in it, cannot pray beyond a certain superficial level. He has no heart to pray. On the other hand, the person whose heart is possessed by the Lord, will grow increasingly in communion with the Lord and, therefore, in prayer.

As we saw, the Lord Jesus desired His Father and went away each morning to meet Him in prayer. Had His heart been possessed by someone else or something else, He would not have found the heart to do what He did. He would have found excuses not to withdraw from people. Although He loved and served people, there is a sense in which the Father was His only love, and that love directed His life.

Today, the people of God are too intimately caught up with the world. They know deep union and communion with the world and the people in it. They desire the company and the presence of things and, by divine law, the love of the Father is not in them. Is it surprising then that they desire the presence of the Lord so little? Is it surprising that after a few minutes in God's presence they do not know what to say, whereas in the presence of men they can talk and talk? Is it surprising that twenty minutes of prayer seems to some as two hours? Is it surprising that prayer is really not the desire of many hearts? Is it surprising that few pay the price of going away to pray, for who wants to go away to spend time with an undesirable person?

The extent to which a person loves to pray alone is an index of that one's love and knowledge of the Lord, for those who love Him hunger and then thirst and finally pant after Him.

If then you would grow in the prayer life, you must separate yourself from all people and all things that possess your heart and let the King of glory reign.

I am worried about a dangerous routine of people who have the idols of things and people in their hearts but who nevertheless have established a prayer programme and accumulated prayer topics and go away and carry out monologues called prayer. I fear because such hearts might sooner or later get hardened towards God and towards sin. I am afraid because such consider themselves as growing in prayer, whereas they are not. None can grow in prayer who did not grow in separation from the lust of the flesh, the lust of the world and the pride of life. None can grow in prayer without a corresponding growth in being delivered from the love of the world and the love of the things of the world.

The one who systemically removes the things of the world and prays, will find that the Lord will systematically move in to occupy the released areas and thus there will be an increase in the love and desire for Him and an increase in the desire for prayer and in the joy of being alone with Him.

Maybe you should stop now and face up to the things and people who occupy your heart. Write them down systematically :

1.
2.
3.
4.
5.

In the name of the Lord Jesus command each person and each

thing to leave God's special throne in you. Insist that each should leave. Beg the Lord to come in at once and occupy the newly released territory. Continue then in prayer and you will make progress.

You may find that the process may need to be repeated because the Lord may further show other occupants of your heart that need to be ousted. You may even find that because of the deceitfulness of your heart some whom you asked to leave the first time did not leave because, although you spoke with your lips that they should depart, you did not release them from your heart for departure. Settle this matter with God and add such to the new list of

1.
2.
3.
4.

people or things or attitudes that must leave the throne of your life so that the Lord Jesus might reign.

Again, as they depart, invite Jesus to take His throne in fullness and reign. Establish the new area for the Lord by increased prayer; so that that newly occupied area of the heart is truly cultivated for the Lord. Praise the Lord!

THE POWER OF ROUTINE

We all like to give the impression that we are original thinkers and that we are not governed by routine. This is actually not the case. Man is actually a routine being. He eats, works, sleeps and does very many things by routine. The body functions by routine. For example, breathing is by a routine function of the lungs, and the heart functions by routine. If any of these routine functions is stopped, there is immediately danger. The crucial thing is whether a man's life functions on the right or the wrong routine. The wise person will establish correct habits in his life and maintain them.

The best of these routines is that which was carried out by the Lord Jesus who in the morning, a great while before day, rose and went out to a lonely place and there prayed.

If you, too, should set out and establish the routine of getting out of bed every morning by or before 4.00 and spending the time before day in prayer alone with God, you will unquestionably become great before Him.

WE INSIST THAT ANYONE WHO WILL PRACTISE THE ROUTINE OF WAKING UP AT 3.45 AM EVERYDAY AND SPENDING THE TIME BETWEEN 4.00 AND 6.00 ALONE WITH GOD IN PRAYER FOR ONE, TWO, THREE... FIVE... TEN...TWENTY YEARS WILL BE UNQUESTIONABLY GREAT BEFORE GOD.

It does not matter what your age or background is, I give you this as one of the best and the most unfailing formulae for success. It worked in the life of the Lord. It must work in your life. However, you will have to follow the formulae in truth and honesty and pay any price that it will take.

You will then, like Jesus, have placed God before man, and that is success. Amen.

9

UNDISTRACTED

"*While he was in one of the cities, there came a man full of leprosy; and when he saw Jesus, he fell on his face and besought him, 'Lord, if you will, you can make me clean.' And he stretched out his hand, and touched him, saying, 'I will; be clean.' And immediately the leprosy left him. And he charged him to tell no one; but 'go and show yourself to the priest, and make an offering for your cleansing, as Moses commanded, for a proof to the people.' But so much the more the report went abroad concerning him; and great multitudes gathered to hear and to be healed of their infirmities. But he withdrew to the wilderness and prayed*" (Luke 5:12-16).

In the previous lesson we saw that the Lord withdrew to pray early in the morning; He withdrew to pray even though crowds had just been healed by Him. In the passage above, we see again that He performed a great miracle. He healed a man who was full of leprosy. He did not want popularity; for He charged the man to tell no one except the priest who had to declare him clean. He did not even tell the man to tell the priest Who had done it. He was simply to tell the priest that before he was leprous but now he was clean.

I am so amazed by the greatness of the Lord Jesus. He had performed a notable miracle. The evidence was there before Him and before many others. He was hated by the religious people. Had He even been a bit in the flesh, He would have told the person to go and show himself to the priest and also to inform the priest that the miracle was performed by Jesus. However, He did not give such instructions. He did not want the popularity that was produced by outward miracles. He wanted a following that had received the inward miracle – the revelation from the Father that He was the Christ.

Today everything that God does is put on the screen so that religious people might profit from them. Those who would tell a man who has received a genuine miracle, "Tell no one," are in very short supply. Because they are really in short supply, God is not able to perform many miracles of the type that our Lord did, in our day. It is not that there is a shortage of people needing miracles. The problem is that there is a real shortage of people who can use God's power exclusively for God's glory. Most will use God's power for the advancement of self, their group, their organization, their denomination, and so on. Since God wants all the glory to be given to the Lord Jesus, He is compelled to withhold His power completely, or limit it severely. May some rise up on the horizons of the Church in this day of great need, who have had all their desire for self-glory dealt with by the cross of Christ and, consequently, are free and available for the Lord, to be used as vehicles through which His power can flow. Lord, do it today. Lord, begin in me.

The Lord Jesus concentrated on His Father. He was the centre of great attraction and great activity, but for Him there was only one attraction – His Father. He healed, He delivered the oppressed, He taught and He did many other things, but there was only one consuming passion in His heart, and that was the desire to be with His Father alone. That is why, after performing the miracle, He closed His heart to the throng that wanted both healing and hearing of the gospel. He had spent the morning, a great while before day with His Father and then He had ministered to this leper. So much was the desire for His Father on His heart that He did the only thing that ought to be done in such situations – He withdrew to the wilderness. All who are under authority are not only accountable. They give account. They take the initiative to give account of what they have done.

TIRED BUT PRAYING

The Lord Jesus must have been tired by the time He healed the leper. The normal reaction expected by most people would have been, "I have done a good job. I have glorified My Father. I have worked. Now I must take My rest, eat and sleep. I must relax."

The Lord did not adopt such an attitude. He might have been tired, but His desire to be with His Father far outweighed His need of rest. Therefore, He went to pray.

Those who will make the most progress with God are those who will give the very early hours of the day to the Lord in prayer and, at the end of the day, instead of just going to sleep, they decide to burn the midnight oil before the Lord, praying. There are times when things are very comfortable and prayer is easy. Such times should be used for prayer. There are other times when the body is tired, broken and weary. It is at such times that a distinction is made between those who pray as a convenience and those who pray as the indispensable 'must' of the day.

The Lord demonstrated by His commitment to prayer that prayer was not only good and necessary but also that it was a 'must' which people neglected to their peril.

The Lord said of the watchmen of Israel, "*All the day and all the night they shall not be silent*" (Isaiah 62:6). A command has gone out to those who love the Lord, "*Take no rest, and give him no rest*" (Isaiah 62:7). Anna prayed and worshipped night and day! Those who would move in the higher spiritual plane are those who have committed themselves to pray in season and out of season, when they are fresh and when they are tired, when they are strong and when they are weak, when they are successful and when all seems to fail, when they are understood and when they are misunderstood.

Every year is prayer year.

Every month is prayer month.

Everyday is prayer day.

Every hour is prayer hour.

There is no time that is bad time for prayer. God is always waiting to be prayed to and He will answer!

THE PRIORITY OF PRAYER

It becomes increasingly obvious that prayer was a priority in the life of the Lord Jesus. It was the one thing that He did at every given opportunity. It seems that to Him, prayer was :

- the first thing,
- the second thing,
- the third thing,
- the last thing.

He prayed because He loved His Father. He also prayed because without prayer He could not go on! He said, "*I can do nothing on my own authority; as I hear, I judge; and my judgment is just, because I seek not my own will but the will of him who sent me*" (John 5:30). He needed to hear what the Father was saying on a daily basis. He sought the Father's will on a daily basis. He put His will aside on a daily basis. He put His opinions aside on a daily basis and He was caught up with the Father on a daily, yearly, hourly basis.

So, whether it was in order to receive power for service or direction for service or plain communion with His Father, the Lord Jesus found the answer in unceasing prayer and He prayed.

He left the presence of man for the presence of His Father.

He left the praise of man for the praise of His Father.

He left the men who wanted to hear more for the presence of His Father where He could hear more.

He left the men who wanted to talk to Him, for the presence of His Father whom He desperately wanted to hear.

He turned His back on the honours and praise that people wanted to shower on Him for His Father's presence, where He could shower praises on Him who gave Him power over diseases.

He withdrew to the wilderness and prayed. He chose a lonely place where He could be undistracted and there He poured out His heart to His Father.

The question may arise in some hearts as to what was the substance of the prayer of Jesus that day as He withdrew from the crowd that wanted both the ministry of miracles and the Word, having seen such a demonstration of power.

I think that the first topic of prayer was His thanksgiving to the Father for allowing His power to flow so wonderfully through Him. The Lord Jesus never took His Father or His Father's power for granted. He knew fully well that all power belonged to His Father and that He could perform miracles because the Father let His power flow through Him. So He must have given thanks. He was utterly grateful. There is no wonder that He was disturbed when He healed ten lepers and only one came back to express gratitude.

How is it like with you? Would you have immediately gone away to give thanks? Would you have decided that there was gratitude that you owed the Father and that you ought to let Him have it alone? Have you ever had anything positive to confess to the Lord which you wanted no human ear to hear? Is the first reaction of your heart to a gift the expression of gratitude? Do you know people to whom you owe gratitude? Will you do something about paying your debt?

I think the second topic of prayer was a request that the Father should reveal Christ to the man He had healed. The man had surely met the Healer, but had he met the Saviour? The Lord Jesus must have pleaded with the Father to save the man.

I think the third topic of prayer was a request that the Father should keep Him from temptation. He was doing exceedingly great things and He was extremely successful. Extreme temptations come to all who are extremely successful, and such temptations come at the moments of maximum triumph. The Lord was well aware of the temptation from Satan that He should abandon the way of the cross and instead win the world through sensational performance. So, the Lord might have prayed, "Father, keep Me in Your love. Keep Me from the evil one. Lord, keep Me looking to the cross as the inevitable way to the throne." By being unpresumptuous the Lord Jesus kept close to the Father and each time the prince of this world came, he had nothing in Him.

The desire to draw attention to oneself after one has been greatly used is there and it is very strong. It is of the flesh and those who yield to it create room for the evil one. May the Lord save you and me from that desire. May the cross do a deep work in us and then we shall be free to be used and used without falling into Satan's trap along the pathway of being used.

I think the fourth thing the Lord Jesus did in prayer was just to give account to the Father of what happened. He was under authority.

REBELS?

One thing seems to begin to crystallize in my mind. It is that the average believer does not know the value of prayer. If the Lord Jesus prayed so much, He who could not afford to waste any time, then prayer must be more central and more potent and more indispensable than most believers know.

The fact that He needed to pray so much in order to be correct about God's will in everything, must say that the average believer who prays so little and knows God and His will so little, must be a rebel, doing his own thing, in his own way and at his own time. It must suggest that there is so little that he is doing which is assuredly the will of God.

God is concerned about the

- who,
- how,
- when,
- with whom,
- for what purpose (reason) of everything.

There is God's perfect timing for everything that ought to occupy a believer's time twenty-four hours of everyday and for all of life. There is no room for the believer to plan and execute his own activities; for everything has been worked out by God, and the planning and execution of man's own plans can only mean that God's plans are left aside either in part or in whole.

This being the case, how can anyone spend so little time in prayer during which he throws a few sentences at God and yet walk in the full counsel of the will of God? That is certainly not possible.

When the Lord comes back, each believer will give account of each thing he did and how each second was used. Those who did not seek the will of God but did many things which they thought were the will of God, will discover on that day that their own activities stood in the way of His. They would have spent much of their lives opposing God, instead of serving Him; for every act of service that is out of tune with His perfect will in any way stands against Him.

The Lord Jesus understood this. He, therefore, sought His Father about everything; for He had to know not only what the Father wanted done, but also the way, the time and the motive for which He wanted it done; if we are going to grow into His likeness, we have no choice but to have recourse to giving the place to prayer that He gave it.

The other thing is that there are things that God says to those who occasionally appear before Him in prayer. There are other things which He says to those who frequent His presence. There are yet other things which He will say to those who have made His presence their dwelling place in prayer; a dwelling place from which they depart to do His will and, as soon as they are through with the activity, return there.

GOD: A DWELLING PLACE

The Psalmist said, "*Lord, thou hast been our dwelling place in all generations*" (Psalm 90:1). "*He who dwells in the shelter of the Most High, who abides in the shadow of the Almighty, will say to the Lord, 'My refuge and my fortress; my God, in whom I trust'*" (Psalm 91:1-2). It is expected that as believers make progress in loving the Lord and in knowing Him intimately, they should draw near increasingly unto Him. They should enjoy His presence exceedingly. His will be the only voice they truly long to hear and His will be the only face they desire to see; His will be the only presence that makes total sense. They will grow into that condition by putting aside all else and cultivating fellowship with Him in His presence. As His becomes the sweetest presence, they will come there again and again and then it will become increasingly difficult to leave His presence. When they must go away in order to carry out some assignment that His gracious will has ordained, they will go out of obedience and not out of pleasure and, as soon as the activity is over, they will run back into His presence, for that is where "home" is.

This is the level of maturity that God expects from those who have known Him for a few years. Unfortunately, this is the maturity that is almost totally lacking in the Church today. His is he maturity of the lovers of the Lord, the maturity of those who will pray and pray and pray and after they have prayed, will begin to pray again: worshipping, listening, hearing, knowing and all else that is involved in the union with God!

This is the maturity to which I aspire. This is the maturity to which you must aspire, so that some day it will not be a matter of recording how much time you spent in prayer, but rather how much time you spent away from prayer.

This is the maturity that was expressed throughout in the life of the Lord. May we draw near to Him and plead with Him; so that He should lead us to this special place in the heart and service of the Lord.

NO SUDDEN JUMP

God is not in the magic business. He will not transform a believer who does not love His presence because he is pregnant with the world and worldly things, into the mature saint we have been describing, without cost, and in one night.

The believer who desires this plane of prayer must actively co-operate by removing the world and worldly things from his heart. It will be painful; for in many hearts the world and what it contains has dug and, like trees, has established strong and deep roots. To uproot such trees will cause pain, bleeding and wounds. It may be the wounds of parting with someone who rivals with God for your heart or the parting with things or the giving away of the pursuits of a cherished worldly position or diploma. It may be the shedding of a place in religious or denominational circles; it may be the forsaking of marriage hopes and so on. You know what it may be in your case. It could even be the call to perpetual material poverty. If you will get rid of all that is illegally enthroned on your heart and all else that is permissible so that the Lord alone might reign there, you will have made a good start.

Then you should begin to spend time in His presence in prayer. From the beginning you may not be very at home, but keep on. You may sometimes not know what to tell Him. Ask Him to teach you how to talk to Him. Plead that He should reveal Himself to you, and show you His glory. Pray that in His love He should bridge the gap that separates you from Him. Ask Him to draw near. Begin to present your needs to Him and ask Him for His opinion about them. Begin to bring to Him names of unsaved people, and plead that He should save them. Begin to bring Him the names of backsliders and plead with Him to restore them to Himself. Begin to bring the names of believers to Him and ask for each that He would create in him a hatred for sin, a deliverance from self and that He should make him grow to be like the Lord Jesus in character, especially in humility and so on. You will find that as you go on in this way, the sense of "strangeness" that used to envelop you when you came into His presence, has begun to disappear and is being replaced by the desire to abide there.

You may want to make rapid progress. If that is the case, you can make a timetable as follows and follow it. Remember, you are learning to be in His presence, to know Him and to talk to Him. Therefore, the more frequent the lessons and the longer each lesson is, the more the chances of success.

WEEK ONE	Monday	thirty minutes
	Tuesday	thirty minutes
	Wednesday	forty-five minutes
	Thursday	forty-five minutes
	Friday	forty-five minutes
	Sartuday	one hour
	Sunday	one hour

WEEK TWO	Monday	one hour
	Tuesday	one hour thirty minutes
	Wednesday	one hour thirty minutes
	Thursday	one hour thirty minutes
	Friday	one hour thirty minutes

	Sartuday	one hour thirty minutes
	Sunday	two hours
WEEK THREE	Monday	two hours
	Tuesday	two hours
	Wednesday	two hours
	Thursday	two hours
	Friday	two hours thirty minutes
	Sartuday	two hours thirty minutes
	Sunday	two hours thirty minutes

WEEK FOUR Draw your own programme depending on the extent to which your appetite for the Lord has grown. If you find that the pace outlined above was too much for you,

modify it, but plead with God that He should enable you to make rapid progress. He will answer you!

10

THE WHOLE NIGHT

"*In these days he went out to the mountain to pray; and all night he continued in prayer to God; and when it was day, he called his disciples, and chose from them twelve, whom he named apostles; Simon, whom he named Peter, and Andrew his brother, and James and John, and Philip, and Bartholomew, and Matthew, and Thomas, and James the son of Alphaeus, and Simon who was called the Zealot, and Judas the son of James, and Judas Iscariot, who became a traitor. And he came down with them and stood on a level place, with a great crowd of his disciples and a great multitude of people from all Judea and Jerusalem and the seacoast of Tyre and Sidon, who came to hear him and to be healed of their diseases; and those who were troubled with unclean spirits were cured. And all the crowd sought to touch him, for power came from him and healed them all*" (Luke 6:12-19).

COMMUNION

Prayer is more than asking and receiving things from God. It is communion with Him. In the course of that communion, the Lord is known, praised and further sought. He then makes His needs known to the praying person and imparts to that one the burden to see the needs of the Lord supplied. Such a one, having thus seen the needs of the Lord, will concentrate on having the needs met. The praying person will only bring up his own needs in so far as the meeting of those needs will help him to meet the needs of the Lord.

The Lord withdrew to the mountain to pray. He needed His Father and His Father needed Him; so He went to be alone with Him. The Lord also had a problem. It was time for Him to set aside twelve of His many disciples as the Twelve: the twelve apostles. He had a great crowd of disciples. Who was He to choose?

He did not depend on how He felt. He did not depend on whom He was attracted to. He did not depend on who apparently held promise for the future. He put aside His opinion and withdrew to have the Father's will on the issue. He went to the mountain to pray. We do not know at what hour He went to the mountain, but we do know that He started to pray and then continued to pray until the whole night was spent in prayer. The issue of selecting the twelve apostles was so serious that there on that mountain, the Divine Council met.

They must have examined each possible candidate and then come to a conclusion that was not based on human wisdom. The God-head established the list and the Son had it. In many ways only God could have chosen that list, for it is a list that defies human explanation. The human viewpoint was left aside completely. There was no thought about regional distribution or representation. There was no thought as to how people would react to it. The men selected did not seem to be all very stable. They each had a character weakness Peter was bold and impulsive. James and John were of a temper that could be destructive. One of them was not even committed to Jesus as Lord; others were timid and so on. When the list was read, there were two sets of brothers; Peter was put ahead of Andrew, even though Andrew came first to the Lord. Two were called James and two were called Judas.

God saw each one of them and knew each one's past, present and future, and yet He chose them. They were to be a difficult lot to train, nevertheless, the Father gave them to the Son and the Son accepted them and committed Himself to them. So the Lord had the list of God's chosen apostles for Him. It had taken the whole night to sort out, for it was one of the most important and most far-reaching choices of all time. The Lord had not decided to spend the whole night in prayer. He had gone to pray and then discovered that the business that He had to settle with the Father required the whole night. He did not shrink from the requirement. He just paid the price and stayed in God's presence until the job was done.

PLANNED LENGTHS OF PRAYER TIME?

If the Lord had said, "I am going away to the mountain to pray for four hours," He would have been in trouble because He would have found out that after four hours the matter that needed to be settled with God was far from settled. He went to meet God and He decided that He would be moved by how long it took to settle all that needed to be settled with God and not by any arbitrary limit of time made by Himself. God never says, "Come to me for one, two or three hours." He invites people to go to Him, and how long they stay is determined by how long it takes to transact the business that needs transaction.

He did call Moses to the mountain. Moses went and entered into God's presence and, before he could come out of there, forty days had gone by. Moses stayed in God's presence until the Lord had finished talking to him. We, too, must make ourselves available to God. We must learn to be perfectly at home in His presence, so that if there is need to spend one hour, ten hours, two days, seven days or forty days, we shall find that we are able to live in His immediate presence for that long.

To be able to stay in God's presence until He has finished talking with us demands that we know Him deeply and have learnt to hear His voice, being able to discern His voice from all other voices and being able to know with accuracy what He is saying. Those who only know how to jump into His presence and rattle a few words of self-initiated need, will find that they are not making the progress they should make.

If a person goes away to pray and continues in prayer all the night because the burden of the Lord was upon him, then that one has made progress.

In addition to the spontaneous times of prayer that may last many hours and perhaps all the night, maturing believers should have planned and programmed nights of prayer. Prayer is a 'must' that should be carried out, regardless of what a person feels like. The Lord has commanded people to pray without ceasing. Those who want to obey Him will pray in the morning, afternoon and evening; they will pray in the day and they will pray at night. They will pray when called apart by the Lord to pray and they will take personal initiative to pray; for all time is prayer time. They will pray throughout the day if they can and when they can, and they will do the same at night. If the Lord does not call them aside to pray, they will invite themselves into His presence to pray.

ALL-NIGHT PRAYER

It is best for the maturing saint to have two all-night prayer meetings of eight to ten hours a week. One prayer night will be a personal prayer night during which he learns to meet God over an extended period alone; it will be difficult from the beginning but, with increasing time, the persevering believer will gain ground in prayer and begin to enjoy the night. It may be that he will start with one prayer night alone once a month and then move on to one every fortnight and finally to once a week.

The prayer night should begin as early in the evening as possible; for a person who works from 08.00-16.00, he might choose to start at 18.00 to 02.00 in order to give himself some time of sleep before going to work the next day.

He might organize his prayer night as follows :

18:00-19:00	Thanksgiving and praise.
19:00-20:00	Prayer for personal needs both material and spiritual.
20:00-20:30	Waiting before the Lord.
20:30-21:30	Praying for the things that were received during waiting on God.
21:30-22:30	Prayer for one's family (both saved and unsaved members).
22:30-23:30	Prayer for the local Church in which one is involved.
23:30-24:00	Praise and thanksgiving in silent songs.
24:00-01:00	Prayer for an unevangelized nation and/or for some ministry of world consequence.
01:30-01:30	Prayer for revival of the saints world over.
01:30-02:00	Thanksgiving and writing down future lines of action.

There will certainly be other ways to organize the all-night prayer session but each person must wait on God and receive from Him what He wants done and how He wants it done. Having received what must be done from the Lord, the praying saint ought to apply himself to it with all diligence, refusing to be called away from it by Satan or by the world or the flesh.

A serious believer will at the beginning of the year already set aside the nights of prayer that he has sorted out with God and protect these with prayer so that the enemy should not interfere. In this way, he will make rapid progress in the knowledge of God and in the release of spiritual power for the accomplishment of God's will.

I consider that every normal local church will have an all-night prayer meeting once a week that will be attended by all the members who are not hindered by some major obstacle. In fact, a normal assembly will only count those who participate regularly at the prayer meetings as its members. The others are visitors. I consider that a large assembly will organize these all-night prayer meetings in homes and that the numbers will be limited to twenty to thirty; so that the number of spectators will be reduced.

The assembly I attend has had a weekly all-night prayer meeting of eight to ten hours once a week for the last ten years. The prayer night I attend at the moment is made up of about thirty believers and we pray once a week from 19.00 to 0.5.00.

As I look into the future, I see this return to all-night prayer meetings in small groups as a sign that the Lord will soon do something great in His Church and through His Church, for when people pray, God moves in might. My prayer is that this matter of praying with the Lord Jesus on a regular basis throughout the night should become ordinary and that wherever redeemed men and women gather together as a local assembly, they should soon give themselves to prayer and to prayer sessions through the night.

THE NIGHT A TIME FOR PRAYER

We know that the evil one is most active in the night. Since he is the prince of darkness, most of his operations are at night. For that reason, all who would stand in opposition to Him must consider praying at night as indispensable to resisting him. It does not sound right to me that we should leave him to do havoc at night and in the day we plead with the Father that He should undo what the Enemy did at night. We must pay the price of being awake and we must resist him. We must take no rest and we must give him no opportunity and then our reward will be great in heaven.

PRAYER AND SPIRITUAL POWER

After the Lord had spent the night in prayer, He received the power to make the right decision to who should be in the group of the twelve. It would seem that He also received a fresh anointing from the Father to perform miracles; for the Bible says of Him shortly after the night spent in prayer that "*Those who were troubled with unclean spirits were cured. And all the crowd sought to touch him, for power came forth from him and healed them all*" (Luke 6:18-19).

There was an extra flow of power because He had been in the presence of the Father. Those who spend time increasingly in prayer grow in spiritual power.

Because power is locked up in prayer, it is difficult to understand why the Church that stands so impotent before a watching world does not do more to pray and release the power of God. Lord, help me to pray more. Lord, help me to solve the matter of my limited spiritual power by a more intense life of prayer. Lord, help me to mobilize the saints to pray. Lord, help me to do all I can to both pray and to move Your children to pray. This is the greatest need of the hour. Lord, help me. Lord, help us.

11

ALONE IN THE MIDST OF OTHERS

"Now it happened that as he was praying alone the disciples were with him; and he asked them, 'Who do the people say that I am?' And they answered, 'John the Baptist; but others say, Elijah; and others, that one of the old prophets has risen.' And he said to them, 'But who do you say that I am?' And Peter answered, 'The Christ of God'" (Luke 9:18-20).

And Jesus answered him, 'Blessed are you, Simon Bar-Jona! For flesh and blood has not revealed this to you, but my Father who is in heaven. And I tell you, you are Peter, and on this rock I will build my church, and the powers of death shall not prevail against it. I will give you the keys of the kingdom of heaven, and whatever you bind on earth shall be bound in heaven, and whatever you loose on earth shall be loosed in heaven" (Matthew 16:17-19).

The Lord Jesus understood the importance of prayer and gave Himself to it. He was not influenced by what others around Him did. He knew what He wanted and He went ahead and did it. The disciples were with Him, but He was praying alone. He was with them, but His thoughts and His being were taken up with His Father. Although He often withdrew to a mountain to pray, He also knew how to pray in the midst of people. There is a sense in which He lived constantly in His Father's presence, even though there was all the crowd around Him.

PRAYING ALONE

One can pray with another person, a group of other people or a crowd of people. There is room in Christian praying for each of these and it should be practised. However, a man's spirituality is not indicated by how much praying he practises in public, but by how much praying he carries out alone. It is possible to walk at a distance from the Lord but pray in public for long periods. However, the state of the heart is most easily revealed when one is alone before God. In that condition, it is as if the eyes of the eternal Father focus on the praying soul and there seems to be no place to hide a backslidden condition. Most people who take time to pray alone at some depth are walking relatively close to the Lord. Those who practise sin find God's presence most detestable.

Each believer must learn to pray alone in addition to whatever praying he can carry out in the midst of others. It is during the sessions of being alone before God that there can be real revelation of the will of God at the personal level. It is also during the periods of being alone before Him that the corruption of the believer's heart is most easily exposed. God respects His children so much that He prefers to correct them individually and not expose their faults to others. It is only when there is no response to that which was shown in private that He sometimes resorts to public exposure.

There are things that lovers can share and talk about in public. There are also things that are reserved for more intimate moments when others are away. Those who love the Lord should seek increasingly to spend time alone with Him. They should consider the time spent alone with Him of greater personal value than that spent in the presence of others. The reality is that although public praying or praying with others has its place, much spiritual growth and progress only take place when a person spends time increasingly before the Lord alone. When such a person afterwards prays in public, there will be something of the freshness and authority that has been built with God in his prayer that cannot be missed.

We believe that the person who wants to grow in a clear knowledge of the Lord Jesus should spend at least half of the time he puts into prayer alone.

THE IMPACT OF HIS PRAYERS

We know that the Lord prayed alone, although we do not know for certain what He asked of the Father. From the events that follow, I think that we can safely say that He prayed that the Father should reveal the Son to one of the apostles. He was later on to pray, "*I thank thee, Father, Lord of heaven and earth, that thou hast hidden these things from the wise and understanding and revealed them to babes; yes, Father, for such was thy gracious will. All things have been delivered to me by my Father; and no one knows the Son except the Father, and no one knows the Father except the Son and anyone to whom the Son chooses to reveal him*" (Matthew 11:25-27).

The confession of Christ by Peter was such a revelation and the Lord Jesus acknowledged that it was revealed to Peter by the Father who is in heaven. The Lord Jesus prayed that Peter should have revelation as to who the Son was. The Father answered and granted the revelation immediately. We ask, "What if the Lord had not prayed?" The most likely thing is that the Father would not have given Peter the revelation. He too might have just said what the people were saying or just kept silent. But thanks be to God, the Lord prayed and the Father worked! The Father is waiting to work if His children would only pray.

There is so much spiritual darkness in the world today. Even in Churches where the gospel is preached regularly there seems to be a veil on many hearts that prevents them from knowing the Lord Jesus. Many make decisions during evangelistic campaigns, but these are mental acknowledgements of Christ without the revelation from the Father. Because there is no revelation, the so-called converts do not last. The fact is that they were never converted;

for the Father did not reveal the Son to them. Even the fact that many believers read the Word yet, do not seem to see or understand the truth in it in such a way that their lives are transformed, all point to the necessity of the Father revealing the Son and revealing the truth in the Word.

If there is going to be a change, there must be an increase in the quality and quantity of prayer for revelation. It would be better for a person to spend five hours a day praying for someone to whom He intends to witness for one hour. A sane evangelist would need to spend five weeks in prayer for every week of evangelistic campaign that is planned. The teacher will need to spend five hours in prayer for every hour of teaching. If this is done, there will be a change. The Father will answer the prayers and reveal the Son to the unsaved. He will hear the prayers and reveal the truth to believers and then they will cease to be hearers only. They will know the truth and it will set them free.

We insist that the Lord must reveal Christ to people and truth to the believer. Without His acts of revelation all preaching, teaching, evangelising, reading of books, listening to cassettes, and the like, are in vain. The carnal mind cannot receive the things of God. They must be revealed to him. This explains why those who attend Churches with a strong prayer life respond more readily to truth from the heart.

The prophet Elisha prayed to the Lord for his servant saying, "*O Lord, I pray thee, open his eyes that he may see*" (2 Kings 6:17). God answered; for the Bible says, "*So the Lord opened the eyes of the young man and he saw*" (2 King 6:17). He also prayed to the Lord for the Syrians, saying, "O Lord, open the eyes of these men, that they may see." The Lord again answered, for the Bible says, "*So the Lord opened their eyes, and they saw*" (2 Kings 6:20).

The apostle Paul was well aware of the fact that only God can grant spiritual sight and spiritual understanding. He therefore prayed that "*The God of our Lord Jesus Christ, the Father of glory, may give you a spirit of wisdom and of revelation in the knowledge of him, having the eyes of your hearts enlightened, that you may know what is the hope to which he has called you, what are the riches of his glorious inheritance in the saints, and what is the immeasurable greatness of his power in us who believe, according to the working of his great might*" (Ephesians 1:17-19).

Have you ever prayed that God should open the eyes of those who have heard the gospel but do not believe in Christ, to see? If you have never prayed that way, why don't you start now? You can make a list of members of your family, your friends, your neighbours, your co-workers and so on, and plead with the Lord that He should open their eyes to see. He will do it and they shall turn to Christ and be saved. You should do the same thing for believers who are in error or who have a mental grasp of some truth but its transforming power is absent from their lives. The Lord will surely hear and cause a new day to dawn in their lives! Praise Him.

LEADERSHIP

We have seen that the Lord Jesus was with the disciples but prayed alone; the disciples did not want to join Him or could not join Him. He, nevertheless, continued in prayer and had results. The leader is the person who will pray when others should not. He will pray long before others join in and, long after others have stopped praying, the leader will continue to press on in prayer.

There is a sense in which the leader is the person who has made the most progress in prayer. The leader is the person who spends the most time in prayer. The leader is the one who is foremost in the quality and quantity of prayer. The apostles as primary leaders had prayer as their foremost task and the ministry of the Word as the second priority.

When a leader has given up on real praying, he has also abandoned leadership. He may use other skills, techniques and gifts to keep the people going with him, but the truth is that he has surrendered leadership by his low quality and low quantity praying.

The Lord Jesus was different. He is the leader indeed. We make Him our example and follow Him into both The School of Prayer and the Ministry of Prayer. We follow Him and pray like Him and, by God's grace, see God reveal Himself to many. Glory be to Him.

Amen

12

PRAYING AND TRANSFIGURED

"Now about eight days after these sayings he took with him Peter and John and James, and went up on the mountain to pray. And as he was paying, the appearance of his countenance was altered, and his raiment became dazzling white. And behold two men talked with him, Moses and Elijah, who appeared in glory and spoke of his departure, which he was to accomplish at Jerusalem. Now Peter and those who were with him were heavy with sleep, and when they wakened they saw his glory and the two men who stood with him. And as the men were parting from him, Peter said to Jesus, 'Master, it is good that we are here; let us make three booths, one for you and one for Moses and one for Elijah' not knowing what he said. As he said this, a cloud came and overshadowed them, and they were afraid as they entered the cloud. And a voice came out of the cloud, saying, 'This is my Son, my chosen; listen to him!' And when the voice had spoken, Jesus was found alone. And they kept silence and told no one in those days anything of what they had seen" (Luke 9:28-36).

THE INNER CIRCLE AT PRAYER

The Lord Jesus was a most wonderful Leader. He is just the perfect example in every way. In the last chapter we found Him praying alone, even though the disciples were with Him but He did not allow things to continue that way. He was anxious that the disciples too should pray. He, therefore, chose the three most prominent ones among the twelve Peter, John and James and went with them on the mountain to pray. He decided that He should first pray with the three before He would pray with the twelve.

The Lord had the inner circle of three disciples to whom He gave more training by exposure to special circumstances, than to the others. He did not choose them because of natural affinity. Rather He chose them with the future of the ministry in mind. Peter was the leader of the team and obviously needed more training than the others. John was the one who would outlive all of them and be involved in the crucial work of restoration when things would begin to fall apart through false teaching and heavy backsliding at the end of the first century. James was the one who was ordained to be the first of the apostles to seal his testimony with his blood. So, these three were critically important and the Lord wanted to ensure that they were prepared for the critical roles that they were going to play in the future. The Lord did not explain to the rest why He had chosen those three. He was not democratic; for, of the three, two were brothers! There are things that a spiritual leader must do and not explain the reasons for doing them to the people he is leading. Those who are being led must allow the leader to do some things without giving them any explanation for them. If he is indeed the leader, he will see some things that they do not see and take appropriate action according to what he has seen. There are things that would disturb those who are led if they are allowed to know them before time.

We have seen that prayer was the priority of priorities for the Lord Jesus. Since that is so, it was only normal that He should take the inner circle away on an on-the-job training in prayer. So He took the three and went with them to the mountain with the specific purpose of praying. He and they knew that the purpose of going to the mountain was to pray.

Leaders must follow the example of the Lord Jesus. They, too, must have an inner circle, depending on the present and future requirements of the ministry. They, too, like Him must not feel obliged to excuse themselves for not giving everyone the same training but, rather, giving some more and thereby making room for grumbling, jealousy and pride. The leader must act and trust the Lord to do a work of dealing with the uncrucified self in both the inner circle and the others. Leaders must decide and take the inner circle away for an evening, a night, a weekend, a week or a season of prayer. This will be part of the best thing he would be doing to prepare them for future leadership; for, should they fail to be leaders in praying and leaders at prayer, they would have no mandate for leadership. WE INSIST THAT THE LEADER MUST TRAIN THE OTHER LEADERS TO PRAY. IF HE TRAINS THEM IN ALL ELSE BUT PRAYER, HE SHOULD CONSIDER THAT HE HAS FAILED, FOR LEADERS WHO ARE NOT ALSO LEADERS IN PRAYING WILL INEVITABLY FAIL.

PRAYING AND TRANSFIGURED

The Bible says, "*And as he was praying, the appearance of his countenance was altered, and his raiment became dazzling white. And behold, two men talked with him, Moses and Elijah, who appeared in glory and spoke of his departure, which he was to accomplish at Jerusalem*" (Luke 9:29-31).

We saw much earlier that as the Lord Jesus was praying the heavens were opened, and the Spirit descended upon Him. So His prayer brought that glorious event to pass. Here, too, we see that it was when the Lord was praying that the appearance of His countenance was altered. Before He prayed, His countenance was unaltered. As He was praying things happened. We conclude that it was the prayers of Jesus that caused the Father to cause His countenance to be altered. Had He not prayed, nothing would have happened.

It was not only His countenance that was altered. His raiment became dazzling white and Moses and Elijah appeared in glory and spoke with Him about His coming death. So we can say that the prayers of Jesus caused the Father to allow the Son to enter into a special experience of pre-resurrection glory. His prayers caused the Father to send Moses and Elijah to Him to, perhaps, comfort Him or give Him some needed information about the far-reaching events that were soon to take place. If the Lord had not prayed, He would probably not have had Moses and Elijah come to Him.

The question must be asked if the Lord asked to be transfigured and for Moses and Elijah to appear in glory with Him on the mountain of transfiguration. We cannot be certain. He might have asked and the Father thus acted in answer to His prayers. On the other hand, it is possible that He did not ask but was rather praying that God's will be done in various areas of His life and ministry. If that is the case, then the Father just caused Him to have that experience and to talk with Moses and Elijah as a bonus. There are things that God will do in answer to prayer. There are many other things which the Lord will do to the praying saint, even though the praying one has not asked for them. If the praying believer is given to labours that the needs of God might be met, he can rest assured that the God of heaven will also ensure that his own needs are met. The Lord will be no one's debtor. Those who serve Him have their needs abundantly met, especially those who serve Him in the very important ministry of prayer. The most blessed people on earth are those who make prayer their business. They receive God's best.

We can see then that the believer who wants to behold the glory of God has to ask for it and it will be shown him. Moses prayed to the Lord, saying, "*Show me thy glory*" (Exodus 33:18). The Lord was glad to answer; for the Bible says, "*And he said, I will make my goodness pass before you, and will proclaim before you my name, 'The Lord'*" (Exodus 33:19).

We can rest assured that those who ask to see His glory will have His glory shown to them, even as it was done to Moses. Generally speaking, the Church today is poor in spiritual experiences.

The primitive Church was different. God was not an intellectual concept but was most manifest in their lives in unmistakable ways. Paul talked of abundance of revelations and so on. Why is it that these things are so much rarer today? There are many reasons for this, but one of the main reasons is the prayerlessness of the Church. It is said of the primitive Church that the apostles gave themselves to the primary duty of praying and the believers as a whole "*Devoted themselves to the apostles' teaching and fellowship, to the breaking of bread and the prayers*" (Acts 2:42). They devoted themselves to the prayers prayer individually, prayer in twos, prayer in small groups, all-night prayer, chain prayer and so on. It was something carried out with devotion. Because they prayed that much, the presence of God was easily manifest in their midst. On one occasion, after they had prayed, the place was shaken and they were all filled with the Holy Spirit. We are not just interested in the shaking of places. However, when people are gathered together in prayer and the place is shaken and that is followed by all of them being filled with the Holy Spirit, then we need the shaking and the filling. Alas, in our day there is often neither the shaking nor the filling but a cold intellectual type of Christianity that does not attract very many, or there is superficial noise made by carnal men. The manifest presence of God is rare or absent because intense praying is rare or absent. We must pray if we are to have manifold spiritual experiences! Will you pray? I will pray!

Because the Lord prayed, the Father sent Moses and Elijah on a special mission to the Son. God always sends special messengers to His praying children. Daniel was a man of prayer and when he was thrown in the lion's den, the Lord sent His angel and shut the lions' mouths. To praying Hananiah, Mishael and Azariah, He sent one like the Son of Man to be their companion in the furnace, and thus saved them from death. YOU WILL KNOW MUCH SUPERNATURAL INTERFERENCE IN YOUR AFFAIRS FOR YOUR GOOD IF YOU WILL GIVE YOURSELF INCREA-

SINGLY TO PRAYER.

SLEEPING DISCIPLES

One of the tragedies of all times is that believers sleep instead of praying. The Lord took the three with Him to go and pray. When they got to the top of the mountain, He was taken up with praying and they, instead of praying with Him, allowed the Enemy to catch them in the web of sleep. The Lord Jesus was caught up with the battle of prayer while they were taken up with the indulgence of sleep. The consequence of this was that while He was clothed in splendour they were clothed with sleep. He was "heavy" with the glory of God and they were heavy with the glory of sleep. He was transfigured but they were not. Moses and Elijah were sent to minister to Him, whereas a voice from heaven rebuked Peter for his stupid talking. Jesus gained everything and they lost everything to sleep.

I do not know if the Lord God had intended that they too should be changed and have a personal foretaste of the glory which shall be the saints' in the Kingdom. If God intended that, then they lost it because of sleep. Could it be that the Lord intended that Moses and Elijah should give them a word of counsel on what they were to do when the Lord would be arrested in the near future? If that was the intention, then they lost it to sleep!

SLEEPING, YOU?

How many times have you slept instead of praying? How many times have you knelt to pray and then just slept off? How often has your prayer sessions turned out to be sleeping sessions? Have you sometimes been made a watchman and, while people were counting on you to pray, you let them down and opened up the entire team to danger because you slept? Do you go to a prayer meeting well dressed up for sleep? Do you choose the seat that will give you a good inclination to sleep? Are you often sleepy when it is time for prayer and then when prayer time is over your sleeping time too is over so that you are awake to do other things?

Sleeping during prayer is evidence of spiritual malady. It says that something is wrong in the sleeper's relationship to His Lord. It should be sorted out at the spiritual level and not taken for a bodily weakness. It is often evidence of the lack of burden and the manifestation of a spirit of laziness. Those who go to prayer meetings and, instead of total preoccupation in prayer spirit, soul and body take a relaxed position and keep quiet, cannot blame the devil for the sleeping session that follows. They wanted it and they have had it. I have noticed over twenty years of leading prayer meetings that it is the same people who sleep at each prayer meeting. I have also noticed that they are people who are generally self-loving and who always seek the cosiest position.

Prayer is war and any soldier who relaxes on the warfront will be taken captive. Those who sleep at prayer are lazy soldiers whom the Enemy has taken captive.

We must also acknowledge that there is a supernatural element with regard to sleep and prayer. We know of disciplined people who take adequate time to prepare by sleeping and eating little or no food and who labour to pray violently, who still find themselves sleeping at prayer meetings, whereas they can spend whole nights doing other things unhindered by sleep. It could be that there are evil spirits that are specially sent by Satan to prayer meetings, charged with the responsibility of causing the saints to sleep instead of praying. This might not be surprising, since that is the weapon of his greatest undoing. I will not be surprised if Satan comes personally to interfere at prayer meetings of consecrated and Spirit-filled believers. If he must do harm, could there be a better place where to operate?

It will be best to bind the devil and cast him and his demons out of every prayer meeting and insist that he should not return.

Such casting would not be superstition. When the sons of God gathered in the presence of God in Job's day, Satan appeared in their midst. He was not afraid to attend a meeting that was personally being led by God. He will not fear to attend a prayer meeting led by you or me today. If he is not to disturb, he and his own must be evicted. We have the mandate to do that. Let us do it and then we shall be freer to pray.

There are a number of other things that should be done to keep awaken. Some people drink stimulants like coffee or tea, others take vitamin C, others eat little or nothing many hours before the prayer meeting. We recommend these things; for they are aids in battle; we also recommend a regular change of posture like praying and walking round and round in a room, and short and long prayer walks of two to twenty kilometres. Finally, we recommend deep and intimate fellowship with the Lord; for this is the final answer to sleeping at prayer.

THE HEAVENS OPEN

The disciples woke up from sleep in time to catch a glimpse of the glory. When they beheld the Lord's glory they ought to have kept quiet. Unfortunately, Peter was not the one to keep quiet. Instead of repenting for his sin of sleeping, instead of praying, he just uttered the next thought that came into his mind. Of course, the thought was not from the Lord. He said, "Master, it is well that we are here; let us make three booths, one for you and one for Moses and one for Elijah" not knowing what he said." People who sleep instead of praying ought to be silent with shame, repent and keep on praying from then on. If they do not do that, they will say things that they ought not to say. Actually, it is those who have prayed who should speak; for they are likely to speak what they have heard from the Lord. Sleeping saints must be silent; I remember a brother who gave himself up to deep sleep at a prayer meeting. When he woke up he told me that he had seen a vision which he wanted to share with the rest of us. I asked him to keep his vision to himself or better still to hand it to the spirits behind sleeping at all-night prayer meetings.

Peter asked that three booths be made: one for the Lord and one each for Moses and Elijah. It was a very wrong suggestion for many reasons: first of all, he was trying to put the prophet and the lawgiver on the same plane with the Lord Jesus. This was so offensive to God that the heavens had to be opened and the Father spoke saying, "This is my Son, my chosen; listen him." There was place only for the Lord Jesus and not for another, and it was the Lord Jesus and not Moses, Elijah or Peter who should speak. Peter and the disciples and all of us ought to bear in mind that when we are before God, we should first listen, hear Him and then convert what we have heard from Him into prayer unto Him. Even in our dealings with the sons of men, it would be good to follow the injunction of James, which says, "*Let every man be quick to hear, slow to speak and slow to anger*" (James 1:19). Secondly, what the disciples intended to do was wrong because they wanted to make permanent something that God wanted to be transient. There are things that should be permanent and we must take sides with God to make them permanent. On the other hand, we must let go that which He has ordained to be passing. The Lord was transfigured for a short time. Moses and Elijah were there for a short time. God's purpose for the event was over and the disciples ought to have seen it that way. Perhaps if they had not been sleeping, they would not have lost God's viewpoint. The Lord was forced to speak from heaven in order to bring their foolish thoughts to an end.

We have written before about the absence of experiences in the Church today, compared to their abundance in the "Primitive" Church. We still encourage believers to ask and receive spiritual manifestations from the Lord. However, no one should try to keep these. They come and they go in a short while and are meant to have lasting impact and strengthen faith. Years afterwards, Peter could write, "For we did not follow cleverly devised myths when we made known to you the power and coming of our Lord Jesus Christ, but we were eyewitnesses of his majesty. For when he received honour and glory from God the Father and the voice was borne to him by the Majestic Glory, "*This is my beloved Son, with whom I am well pleased,' we heard this voice borne from heaven, for we were with him on the holy mountain*" (2 Peter 1:16-18). However, the physical manifestations are not meant to abide. May God deliver us from trying to establish and render permanent that which is meant to be passing. May He enable us to listen to Him and do what He tells us to do. Then we shall be saved from error.

The heavens were opened to exalt the Lord and rebuke the disciples. This was again the fruit of the prayers of the Lord; for He prayed while the disciples slept. The heavens will open when praying people ask the Lord to open them. They will also be opened at the Father's initiative to bless a praying man. Finally, they will open to silence those who want to belittle the authority and glory of a praying man.

No praying man should bother to defend his honour or position. God is well able to do that, and He always does it.

SHORT PRAYERS

We have already written on the need to have each activity preceded by five-fold praying. We wrote that as an encouragement to persistent labours in prayer. No one should understand us as saying that God will only work if there has been a five-fold ministry in prayer. There will be short prayers that last less than two minutes that will receive immediate answers. The Lord has promised to answer before we call. The person who is given to the ministry of praying should expect God to move in might and give him the things that were systematically asked for in prayer as well as those which were asked on the spur of the moment.

Let us make up our minds to always ask and the Lord be given the freedom of granting our request when His heart is satisfied, be it after one minute or ten years of praying. Glory be to His holy name.

13

THANKSGIVING AND WORSHIP

"In that same hour he rejoiced in the Holy Spirit and said, 'I thank thee, Father, Lord of heaven and earth, that thou hast hidden these things from the wise and understanding and revealed them to babes; yea, Father, for such was they gracious will. All things have been delivered to me by my Father; and no one knows who the Son is except the Father, or who the Father is except the Son and anyone to whom the Son chooses to reveal him'" (Luke 10:21-22).

THE REJOICING OF MAN

There are many things that cause man to rejoice. They could range from a good meal, increase in salary or even the misfortune of an enemy. In the preceding event, the Bible says, "*The seventy returned with joy, saying, 'Lord, even the demons are subject to us in your name!' And he said to them, 'I saw Satan fall like lighting from heaven. Behold, I have given you authority to tread upon serpents and scorpions and over all the power of the enemy; and nothing shall hurt you. Nevertheless, do not rejoice in this, that the spirits are subject to you; but rejoice that your names are written in heaven'*" (Luke 10:17-20).

The joy of the disciples was the joy of ordinary men. They rejoiced because "Even the demons are subject to us in your name."

They rejoiced because they could exercise power over evil spirits. Their joy could be illustrated as follows:

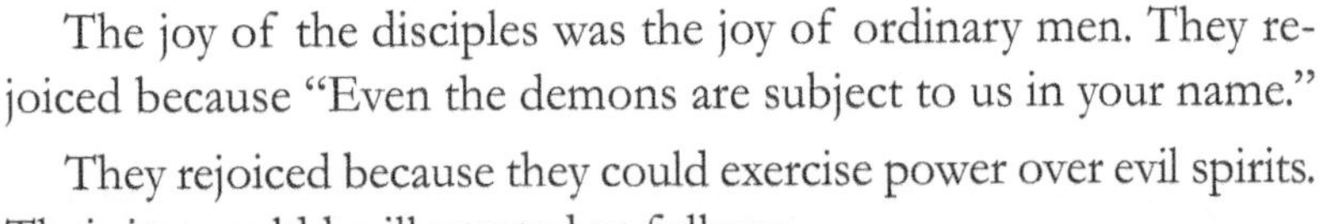

Their joy was, as such, dependent on what they did. It was dependent on something that needed to be repeated again. Their joy meant that as far as demons remained and they could encounter them and cast them out, their joy would remain. However, if there would be no more demons to cast out, even if they abode in the Lord and were faithful, their joy would be finished. Their joy could, as such, not be guaranteed; for it needed an increasing availability of demons to be cast out and an undiminishing power to cast them out. It is true that the casting out of demons was a fruit of their obeying Christ, but He never intended that their joy should depend on something outward, something changeable.

The Lord Jesus told them to rejoice instead in the fact that their names were written in heaven. In that case their joy could be illustrated as follows:

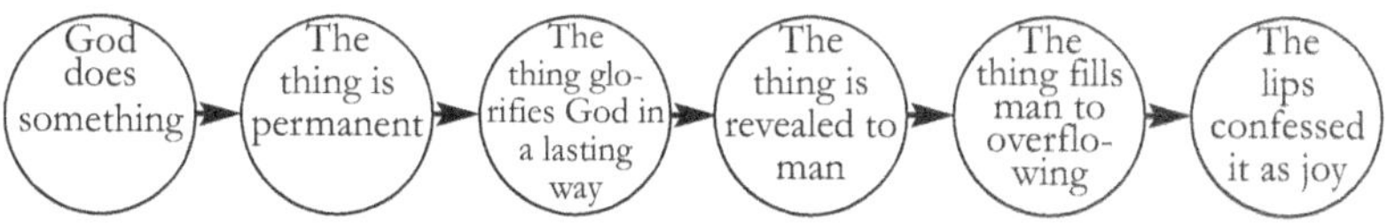

Joy that is based on this kind of foundation is permanent. It is always there. No one who has this kind of joy need ever be sad. The extremes of abundant excitement today and abundant sorrow or being cast down tomorrow, are eliminated.

The joy to which the Lord Jesus called the disciples is joy that exalts the Father and the Father alone. In rejoicing in the fact that they were able to cast out demons, they reported, "Lord, even the demons are subject to us in your name." The "us" is significant. The joy that the Lord Jesus gives, His joy, is that which "decentralizes self" and that puts the Father on the throne. Take, for example, if they were to rejoice because their names were written in heaven, they would always rejoice, but there would be no room for self-exaltation; for who could boast because the Lord has written his name in heaven?

True rejoicing is that which comes out of a situation in which

God receives all the glory. In every situation we are to ask, 'Where is the glory of God in this?" If there is no obvious glory of God, then that cannot be the source of God-ordained joy for us.

THE REJOICING OF THE LORD JESUS

The Lord Jesus did not rejoice in the flesh. He rejoiced in the Holy Spirit. His rejoicing had its origin in the Holy Spirit. It resulted in praise to the Father. It resulted in thanksgiving to the Father. It was the fruit of what the Father had done. It was not the fruit of what the Son had one. It was the Father, the Father, the Father from start to finish. He rejoiced and said, "I thank thee Father, Lord of heaven." He then thanked the Father for what would have caused many people to be angry with the Father the fact that the Father had hidden these things from the wise and understanding and revealed them to babes. He rejoiced because that was the Father's gracious will, because it was well-pleasing before the Father. This gracious will of the Father meant that the wise and the understanding did not believe in the Son but stood in opposition to Him. The Father ordained it that way and the Son was fully satisfied with it. That gracious will meant that only babes believed and followed Him, and He rejoiced in that.

How contrary to man that was! How contrary to many of us that is! He rejoiced in the fact that there could be no random knowing of the Father or of the Son. He rejoiced in the fact that men could not come to Him or know the Father on their own. God had to do it. So, He rejoiced in a situation where God had absolute authority as to who could know Him.

Earlier on He had said, "*Woe to you, Chorazin! Woe to you; Bethsaida! For if the mighty works done in you had been done in Tyre and Sidon, they would have repented long ago, sitting in sackcloth and ashes. But it shall be more tolerable in the judgment for Tyre and Sidon than for you. And you, Capernaum, will you be exalted to heaven? You shall be brought down to hades*" (Luke 10:13-15).

These situations that He had just cited would have discouraged most people and led to despair. It was a sign that they had rejected Him and His message. However, He did not despair. He was not discouraged. He did not want to give up. He turned to the Father and He rejoiced in the Father, thanking and blessing Him for His gracious will, which included His rejection. The rejoicing of the Lord Jesus could be illustrated as follows:

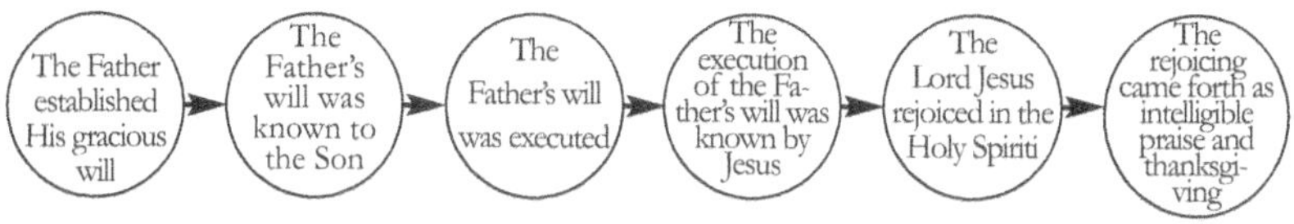

The rejoicing of the Lord Jesus depended unconditionally on the will of the Father. As far as that will was manifested, the Lord rejoiced and blessed the Father for it. Even when that will meant that people turned away from Him and His ministry appeared like a failure before man, He rejoiced and gave glory and thanksgiving to the Father.

John the Baptist knew such an experience. The Bible says, "*Now a discussion arose between John's disciples and a Jew over purifying. And they came to John, and said to him, 'Rabbi, he who was with you beyond the Jordan, to whom you bore witness, here he is, baptizing, and all are going to him.' John answered, 'Now one can receive anything except what is given him from heaven. You yourselves bear me witness, that I said, I am not the Christ, but I have been sent before him. He who has the bride is the bridegroom; the friend of the bridegroom, who stands and hears him rejoices greatly at the bridegroom's voice; therefore this joy of mine is now full. He must increase, but I must decrease'*" (John 3:25-30).

The people were turning away from John and going to Jesus. This was God's gracious will, and John rejoiced greatly in it. His joy came to the fullest when people turned from him to the Lord Jesus. As they turned, it gave room for Jesus to increase before man and for John to decrease. His was true joy. His was true rejoicing. Who or what could take it away from him? He rejoiced at the opportunity to decrease, who would take away his joy?

THE BELIEVER'S REJOICING

God has called the believer to rejoice always. He has called him to rejoice in the Lord. How can this be worked out simply and practically? It can be worked out by using the words of "joy" as follows:

Jesus first,

Others next,

Yourself last.

The person who will put Jesus first in all the situations that come his way, and others next and himself last, will maintain unchanging joy. That is what John the Baptist did. He put the Lord Jesus first. He wanted Him to increase while he, John the Baptist decreased. He acted to bring that to realization. Secondly, he put the disciples who were with him and the crowd that was with him next. Their best interest was that they should follow Jesus instead of him and he led them to Jesus. Then he thought about himself last. There was a place for him and that place was by the Bridegroom, and he took it with rejoicing. Those who will not practise "joy" are practising "Yoj." "Yoj" is:

You first,

Others next,

Jesus last.

All the sin in the world is the fruit of people living out of "yoj" instead of "joy." The Holy Spirit produces joy, but before He can produce it in a person, He must decentralize the self in the person so that instead of the person putting himself first, he puts Jesus first, others next and himself last.

The simple formula of "joy" when practised, will revolutionalize the world by revolutionalizing the lives of individuals, families and communities. Will you give it a try?

WHAT HAS ALL THIS GOT TO DO WITH PRAYER?

You may be asking how all this fits into the book. Well, it fits in because Jesus prayed when He turned to the Father and said to Him, "*I thank thee, Father, Lord of heaven and earth, that thou hast hidden these things from the wise and understanding and revealed them to babes; yes, Father, for such was thy gracious will…*" (Luke 10:21-22). Thanksgiving is prayer. Thanksgiving is an exalted form of prayer. It is the expression of gratitude. Those who can thank the Lord in all circumstances are truly mature; for to do that means that the cross has done a deep and fundamental work in them. Some will thank the Lord if He does the things that advance their "self-life." However, to thank the Lord when the "self-life" is being brought to naught, is progress. Job, at the moment of great loss, said, "*The Lord gave, and the Lord has taken away, blessed be the name of the Lord*" (Job 1:21). That is costly praise. It is sacrificial praise and we are called to offer it to the Lord. The Bible says, "*Through him then let us continually offer up a sacrifice of praise to God, that is the fruit of lips that acknowledge his name*" (Hebrews 13:15).

The Bible expects the believer to give thanks to the Lord in everything. For example, "*Give thanks in all circumstances; for this is the will of God in Christ Jesus for you*" (1 Thessalonians 5:18). "*Always and for everything giving thanks in the name of our Lord Jesus Christ to God the Father*" (Ephesians 5:20). "*And whatever you do, in word or deed, do everything in the name of the Lord Jesus, giving thanks to God the Father through him*" (Colossians 3:17). The Lord Jesus left us an example of this. We should follow in that example. The Lord is in absolute control. We must not judge things by their surface value. We must trust Him and in all circumstances give thanks to the Father through Him. The worst will never happen to us. God, and not the devil, is in ultimate control. God will accomplish His Word, which says, "*We know that in everything God works for good with those who love him, who are called according to his purpose*" (Romans 8:28). Another rendering of the verse says, "*We know that everything works for good with those who love him, who are called according to his purpose*" (RSV margin). Yes, everything must work for the good of all who are called according to His purpose. What is that purpose? That purpose is that "Those whom he foreknew should conform to the image of his Son, in order that he might be the firstborn among many brethren." We thank the Lord for anything and for everything that will enable us to conform to the image of Christ. God is working in every situation, regardless of how we see it now, to accomplish that end. Therefore, even when we cannot understand, we must believe the Word and thank Him for the good that is coming.

Someone may ask, "What of the plans and the activities that are aimed at destroying God's work and destroying us?" The answer is that the devil is not final. God is final. The plans of the devil that are geared against us are often turned to our good to the praise of God's name. Those of his plans that God cannot turn to our good and His praise, He frustrates and brings to naught. Because often the devil uses men, the Bible expresses this truth by saying, "*Surely the wrath of men shall praise thee; the residue of wrath thou wilt gird upon thee*" (Psalm 76:10). So there is the wrath that becomes a source of praise to the Lord and there is the residue of wrath that the Lord girds upon Himself. We are then sure that the devil will not be allowed to bring anything against us that we cannot turn to the praise of God.

Let us then praise and thank the Lord in every circumstance and, thereby, prove that we have learnt from Christ. Amen.

14

THE BATTLE FOR MISSIONS

"*After this the Lord appointed seventy others, and sent them on ahead of him, two by two, into every town and place where he himself was about to come. And he said to them, The harvest is plentiful, but the labourers are few; pray therefore the Lord of the harvest to send out labourers into his harvest*" (Luke 10:1-2).

THE PLENTEOUS HARVEST

The Lord Jesus said that the harvest is plenteous. What harvest is there which is plentiful today? First of all, there is the harvest of your total person spirit, soul and body for the Lord. This is the first harvest that the Lord wants. He wants our co-operation; so that He may reap this harvest of the total man before He can lead us to do anything else for Him. Secondly, there is the harvest of your family. He wants that every member of your family should come to Him and render Him total obedience in everything. Until that happens, there is plenteous harvest in your family. Thirdly, there is the harvest of your neighbours. He desires that your neighbours: those who live close to you, those who work close to you, those who travel close to you should all come to Him and render to Him total obedience in all things.

Fourthly, there is the harvest of your city, town or village. He wants all the people there to hear the gospel, and to come to the Lord Jesus and render to Him total obedience in all things. Fifthly, there is the harvest of your nation. That, too, is plenteous. He wants the people of your nation to hear of His redeeming love and respond to it and turn to Christ and render to Him total obedience in all things. Sixthly, there is the harvest of your continent. God has divided the world into continents. In fact, continental identity seems more logical than national identity. He wants a rich and abundant harvest in your continent. And lastly, you are after all a human being and there are human beings all over Planet Earth. You are after all a world Christian. You belong to the faith in Jesus Christ which is being proclaimed and which needs to be proclaimed the world over.

Looking at it this way, there is a harvest of over five billion people on planet Earth that is waiting. In many places the harvest is ripe, perhaps overripe and might soon be ruined for shortage of labourers. Yes, there is a harvest that is plentiful.

THE HARVEST IS HIS

The seven-fold harvest of yourself, your family, your neighbours, your city, your nation, your continent and your planet, is God's harvest. This must be understood very clearly. The harvest does not belong to some individual, ministry, organization, denomination, nation or continent. The harvest is the Lord's. The Father is the Lord of the harvest. It is His harvest.

For anyone to claim anyone, any place, any city, any people and so on as belonging to them or to their work, is folly. If any part of the harvest belongs to man, it cannot be God's. Anyone who claims a part of the harvest for himself, is also saying that that part of the harvest is not God's. If I label a part of the harvest as mine, I also separate it from God.

All who think that they are serving the Lord need to stop and ask, "Whose harvest is it?" To try and exaggerate the differences between us and the others who truly know and love the Lord, is to say that we have a harvest of our own that we want to protect. To try to own men is to do a very sinful thing. To tell people, "If you are to continue with me, do not have any fellowship with the other brethren," is to cause harm. Even when a part of the body has seen an aspect of the truth that the others have not seen, those who have seen that aspect of the truth must not forsake that which they have seen. They must uphold it and enter into an ever-increasing experience of it. However, they must uphold it in full knowledge of the fact that it is only an aspect of the truth and that they have other aspects of the truth to discover. They must practise the truth that they have received in humility, counting those who have not yet seen that aspect of the truth as better than themselves. They must practise the truth that they have seen in humility and meekness of heart, endeavouring to maintain the bond of unity in love. In this way they acknowledge that the harvest is not theirs. It belongs to Another. It belongs to the Lord.

We repeat that all the five billion people on planet Earth today belong to the Lord. All the mission fields of Africa, America, Australia, Europe and Asia belong to the Lord. They belong to the Lord alone. They do not belong to the Catholic, Presbyterian, Assemblies of God, Methodist or any denomination that you can think of. They do not belong to the Evangelistic Mission to the East, West, North, or South. They do not belong to Youth with a Mission, Open Doors, or any of these tools that God has graciously used and is using. They belong to the Lord. They are the Lord's.

It may be that all who belong to the Lord ought to come to Him in a definite act of surrender and give back His harvest which they have been trying to own for themselves. It may be that now is the moment to go before the Lord with what you call your work, ministry, church, people, area, mission, denomination, and hand it to Him, saying to Him, "Lord, take it all. The harvest is Yours. It was never mine but I have made as if it was mine and I have done great harm. That harvest shall from this day and forever be Yours. I will never again possess what is Yours. You possess me."

THE LABOURERS ARE FEW

It is striking that the Lord should have complained about the quantity of labourers then. It is even more striking that He must be making the same complaint today with so many people calling themselves His. (There are about 50 million people in the USA who claim to be born again. Are these 50 million labourers? The same fabulous numbers are given for many countries in Asia, Africa and Latin America.) There can be many converted people in a place, yet labourers are absent. Labourers are few because of what it takes to be a labourer. A labourer is one who:

1. is thoroughly converted,
2. is filled with the Holy Spirit,
3. has said a final good-bye to sin in all forms and all its manifestations,
4. has said farewell to the love of the world and the love of the things that are in the world in one act of radical abandonment that is renewed every day,
5. has seen that the harvest is the Lord's and the Lord's alone,
6. is prepared to leave all that he has and all that are his to obey the call of God to go anywhere in the harvest that the Lord chooses for Him,
7. is prepared to work hard at the harvest, doing nothing to spare himself.

People who meet the requirements above are rare. There is a real shortage of labourers. We can just look at the instructions that were given to the seventy and ask how many people are prepared to go today on these terms:

1. Carry no purse; no bag, no sandals, and salute no one on the road.
2. Whatever house you enter, first say, "Peace be in this house."
3. Remain in the same house, eating and drinking what they

provide.

4. Heal the sick.

There are three types of labourers who can be "sent":

1. Those who will go physically.
2. Those who will go through their prayers.
3. Those who will go through their giving.

For each type of labourer, the radical conditions of discipleship must be met, which include what Jesus said when He proclaimed, "*If any man would come after me, let him deny himself and take up his cross daily and follow me*" (Luke 9:23), and "*So therefore, whoever of you does not renounce all that he has cannot be my disciple*" (Luke 14:33).

The labourer who goes to preach the gospel of the Crucified Lord must be a crucified man. The labourer who prays must be a crucified man in order to be able to pray for the ministry of crucified men. The labourer who gives must be a crucified man who is living a life of daily renouncing of everything. If not, he cannot truly give to meet the needs of crucified men who are on the battlefront.

THE ANSWER TO A SHORTAGE OF LABOURERS IS PRAYER

God's answer to the shortage of labourers is so different from what takes place today. Man has set up various systems to rapidly fill people's heads with Bible information and then send them out into man's harvest. People of questionable character, consecration and sanctification are sent out to go and labour. They go out to labour for the one who sent them man.

God has one answer to the shortage of labourers. That answer is prayer to the Lord of the harvest. So we have whom to pray to, what to pray for and who may pray.

Prayer is to God the Father. He is the Lord of the harvest.

Prayer is by labourers. It was to the seventy, to those who were qualified to go that the Lord asked that they pray for labourers. He did not ask the multitude to pray. He asked those who met His qualifications as labourers to pray for other labourers.

If a man who has not denied and is not denying himself, who is not taking up his cross daily and who has not renounced all that he has, decides to pray, he is doing great harm. He is asking that God should raise people whose hearts are like his and send them into His harvest. If God heard that prayer, He would have to send out unqualified people into His harvest. Such praying is sin.

If a person knows that there is a shortage of labourers, he should first ask himself, "Am I a labourer? Can God send me out? If God sent people whose hearts are like mine, would it advance the harvest before God or hinder it?" On a careful examination, he may find that he is not qualified to be sent as a labourer and is, consequently, disqualified to pray for labourers. If he yet wants to be useful for the Lord, he will set out to pray that the Lord of the harvest should make him fit to be a labourer in the harvest. He will bring his whole life before God and obtain God's verdict about it. He will then labour with the Lord to put that which is wrong right. After he has put things right, he will qualify as a labourer, and God will then "send" him out to pray for labourers.

The spiritual requirements in terms of purity, holiness and consecration that are required from those who labour by going or labour by praying or labour by giving, are exactly the same. The unconsecrated donor is doing the Gospel enterprise harm. His money will lead people to carry out projects that God has not authorized or cause people whom God has not sent out to go out and, as such, stand in the way of God.

PRAYING FOR LABOURERS

We have said that for an unconsecrated person to pray that God should raise and send out consecrated labourers, is to practise falsehood. God cannot use my prayers to do in the life of another person what I have not let Him do in my life. God cannot use a man beyond the level of his consecration.

Because there are so few in the Church whose hearts are pure and consecrated, the task of praying for labourers must remain the work of the very few. If you are one of those few, the following paragraph is for you.

You are important to God; you are needed by God. You are precious to Him. You belong to a rare class. The devil hates you. The devil will like you to compromise, fall into sin or into worldliness and be disqualified. You should therefore walk very close to the Lord and take no chances. Hate sin with all your heart. Love the Lord with all your heart. Hate falsehood with all your heart. Love the truth with all your being.

Make yourself available to the Lord. Formally tell Him, "Lord, here I am. I am prepared to go into Your harvest. I place myself at Your disposal. I am prepared to be a 'going', 'praying' or 'giving' labourer. Show me where You have placed me." He will show you. He hears and He answers and He will show you.

If He makes you a going labourer, accept it with gratitude and ask Him what you should do in order to prepare to go. Also ask Him where He wants you to go to. As you prepare and as you go, you should know that you have the responsibility to pray not only for yourself and the field to which He is sending you but also to pray that other labourers should be found for other fields. When you get to your field of service, continue to pray that the Lord should send forth labourers into His harvest. So you will labour at your field with one hand and with the other, labour at praying that God should send forth labourers into His harvest.

If He makes you a "praying" labourer, you must give yourself in a more definite way to praying, both for more labourers and for those labourers who are already on the field. Wait before the Lord and receive instructions from him as to how you are to pray. He may want you to invest your life in praying for an unreached tribe or people. Concentrate mainly on that. Block those people from self-appointed or man-appointed labourers who might rush there and destroy the harvest. Plead that God should act quickly and prepare and send His own labourers there. Pray that would-be labourers who are still bound by sin or the love of the world should be released from these and made ready for appointment by God. Plead with God to release labourers who are being blocked from being made available by parents, relatives and social systems. Plead with God to move governments that make entry difficult. Pray that God should touch the hearts to whom the labourers are ministering and will be ministering. Pray that there should be a revelation of Christ and a revelation of His Word. Pray that young converts should desire the sincere milk of the Word and that they should grow. Pray that those who are converted should soon grow and become teachers. The Lord will lead you. Pray also that "giving" labourers should be raised. Pray that the Lord should protect the hearts of the "giving" labourers from the love of money. Pray that the Lord should bless their resources; so that they will have more to give. Protect the resources of the "giving" labourers from attacks by the wicked one. Plead with God that He should multiply the resources and make them enough for the work. Pray that the "giving" labourers should be kept from the seduction of projects that are not of the Lord's creation. Pray that they should be kept from trying to imitate the lifestyle, methods and goals of other people in the vicinity who are actually the labourers of men sent out into the harvest of men.

There is so much to pray about that, were you to give yourself to twenty-four hours of praying a day, you would not be able to pray for all that needs to be prayed for.

If you are a "praying" labourer, you are not exempted from giving sacrificially and not exempted from "going" within the limits where God has sent you.

DESPERATE NEED

We live on the eve of Christ's return. There is still so much that must be done. May the people of God arise, put all sin and all worldliness aside and consecrate themselves totally to the Lord and, thereby, qualify as labourers; so that God will have millions to go, pray and give and then the task will soon be finished and the Lord Jesus will come. Amen.

PART 2

JESUS' SCHOOL OF PRAYING

15

THE ONE THING THAT NEEDED TO BE TAUGHT

"*He was praying in a certain place, and when he ceased, one of his disciples said to him, 'Lord, teach us to pray, as John taught his disciples*" (Luke 11:1).

Again we find the Lord Jesus at prayer. Prayer was so much His way of life that at the slightest opportunity, He resorted to prayer. Those who know God deeply and have found their dwelling place in Him will do the same. If they have an hour before them, they will withdraw and pray. If they have thirty minutes, they will do the same. And if there are only fifteen, ten, five or one minute before them, they will still use it for prayer. Actually, one minute is a lot of time. I have often used one-minute periods to thank the Lord for our children. Since there are six of them, I spend ten seconds on each child and thank the Lord for one thing that He has done in the life of the child. In the next minute, I make six requests to the Father in the name of Jesus, one for each child. Then in another one minute, I build a wall of protection round some area of the life of each of the children. So there is so much that can be done with short periods of time as the Lord used time to pray.

In the incident before us, we are told that He was praying in a certain place. Every place was a prayer place for Him. He could pray everywhere and anywhere. Actually, if He was to obey the Scriptural injunction that says, "*Always and for everything giving thanks in the name of our Lord Jesus Christ to God the Father*" (Ephesians 5:20), then He had to be able to pray anywhere, and He did.

The striking thing is that the disciples were in that place but they did not join Him in prayer. They let Him pray alone. This time they were not sleeping. Then they did something. They asked Jesus to teach them to pray.

These men had already been with the Lord Jesus for nearly three years. He had called them together and given them power and authority over all demons and power to cure diseases, and then sent them out to preach the Kingdom of God and to heal. They had obeyed and gone as He had sent them and preached the Gospel everywhere and healed everywhere. They had preached without asking to be taught to preach. They had healed without having been taught to heal and they had cast out demons without being taught to cast them out. They had done all these things without having prayed. They had done all these things without knowing how to pray.

It becomes evident that a person can preach, teach, heal and cast out demons without having prayed! It means that a person can do all these things without knowing how to pray. It means that it is easier to preach, teach, heal and cast out demons than it is to pray; for, the more difficult a thing is, the more difficult it is to learn it without careful and systematic teaching.

The disciples had seen the Lord pray and observed that the Father answered Him. They knew that He often withdrew and then talked to the Father, but they could not imitate Him. It was possible to imitate Him in all the other things except this one.

I understand why the disciples could not learn to pray just by imitating the Lord. Prayer is not just withdrawing to a lonely place. Prayer is not just throwing some words of thanksgiving or praise or request to the Father. Prayer is communion with God. It is the pouring of oneself to God. It is the reception of the needs of God into one's spirit, and a labour to ensure that God moves and answers those needs.

If prayer were a monologue, the disciples would easily have learnt it, but communion is something that cannot be entered into by doing the outward things that another person is observed to be doing. The inward touch, the inward flow plus the outward acts constitute communion, but the heart of it is the inward touch, and that cannot be faked.

The disciples had not yet known the Father. Some time after this incident they asked Jesus, "*Lord, show us the Father, and we shall be satisfied*" (John 14:8). Since prayer is communion with the Father and they did not know the Father, it is understandable that they could not pray. Those who do not know the Father cannot really pray. Since only the Son can reveal the Father, only those who have been to the Son and have had Him reveal the Father to them can truly pray to Him. This must mean that, although those who are outside Christ have long sessions of real meditation and much speaking, it is not communion with God. They do not know the Son and, consequently, have no revelation of the Father and, as such, cannot pray. Meditation can be a matter of controlling the human mind and bringing it into focus. It could even be the release of the human spirit by man. However, none of these is prayer. Prayer is the release of the human spirit by the Holy Spirit Godward. Consequently, true prayer is a function of redeemed men, and even redeemed men need to be taught how to pray.

THE HONESTY OF THE DISCIPLES

We thank the Lord that the disciples were honest. They did not hide their ignorance. They did not give the impression that they knew what they did not know. There are many believers today who are where the disciples were. They do not know how to pray. They may throw a few words at God to express some need or rattle a few sentences in tongues, but they do not know how to pray to God! Such believers may be people who believed one, three, five or ten years ago! They may be preachers, teachers, Sunday School teachers, evangelists or pastors, but they do not know how to pray. They may be graduates from Bible Schools and may have degrees and even doctorate degrees in theology or the Bible, yet they do not know how to pray. They have never been taught how to pray. They have never been honest enough to own up, saying, "I do not know how to pray. I must find someone to teach me how to pray."

If you are one such person who does not know how to pray, do not give up. There are many like you. You are just like the disciples were after three years with Jesus. They had carried out distinctive ministry in the areas of preaching and miracles, but they had not known how to pray! They asked and were taught how to pray. You, too, can ask and be taught how to pray. The Lord Jesus was there to receive their request and to grant it. The Holy Spirit is here to receive your own request and to grant it. He may teach you Himself or He may send you to some member of the body of Christ who will teach you, on His behalf, how to pray. ALL WHO ASK TO BE TAUGHT HOW TO PRAY AND WHO INSIST THAT THEY BE TAUGHT AND ARE WILLING TO LEARN, WILL BE TAUGHT HOW TO PRAY.

On the other hand, those who do not know how to pray but lack the humility to expose their ignorance and ask to be taught how to pray, will remain in their dangerous ignorance. Those who do not know how to pray but have deceived themselves or allowed themselves to be deceived that they can pray and, consequently, do not ask to be taught to pray, will continue in their self-deception. They have only themselves to blame.

Permit me to ask you a question, "Do you know how to pray?"

The answer to that question and what you do about it can make a difference to your spiritual life, your ministry and your heavenly rank. Be careful to answer this question honestly. Be careful to do something about the honest answer, should you need to do something about it. Do not let the pride of position or years in the Lord deceive you or force you to deceive yourself. You know what the truth is!

16

JESUS GAVE THEM WHAT TO SAY

"And it came to pass, as he was praying in a certain place, when he ceased, that one of his disciples said to him, 'Lord, teach us to pray, as John taught also his disciples.' So he said to them, 'When you pray, say: Our Father in heaven, hallowed be Your name. Your kingdom come. Your will be done on earth as it is in heaven. Give us day by day our daily bread. And forgive us our sins, for we also forgive everyone who is indebted to us. And do not lead us into temptation but deliver us from the evil one'" (Luke 11:1-4, KJV.)

The disciples asked the Lord to teach them how to pray. The Lord did not rebuke them for their ignorance. He did not say to them, "What have you been doing all these years? Why did you not ask earlier? Have you not seen Me at prayer? Did you not hear what I said to My Father and how I said it? Did you not see the way He answered?" The Lord was rather glad that they had asked. He must have been waiting for that moment when their eyes would be opened to the vital importance of prayer and they would want to be taught. The Lord knew that no one could force another person to want to pray. He knew that the desire had to come from the heart; that God had to put it there. It could be that in His prayer to the Father just before their question, He was pleading with the Father to cause them to ask to be taught. There are issues over which a teacher must prayerfully wait until the pupil or student is ready to learn the lesson. He cannot just pour out things at his own pace. He must aim at permanent impact. When the disciples were ready and asked, the Lord Jesus went to their aid. He did not postpone it. He did not do other things before He came to it; he knew the priority, the importance, as well as the urgency of prayer, so He could wait no longer!

Has someone ever asked you to teach them to pray? Has someone ever asked to pray with you so as to learn from you? How did you react? Did you encourage the person as clear evidence that you know the importance of prayer or did you postpone it, give it a secondary place until the desire died away? When you found someone who was desirous to learn to pray, did you encourage the person and prayerfully protect the desire in his heart so that Satan might not snatch it away or did you do nothing about it?

The Lord Jesus decided to teach His disciples to pray. It is interesting to note three things :

- How He taught them,
- What He taught them,
- The order in which He placed things, that is, the priorities that He had in mind.

These three things should guide us in our own praying and in the teaching of any people who might want to learn from us.

Jesus taught them what to say. He did not say to them, "When you pray, include the Father's interests and your personal needs and your safety." He told them, "When you pray, say." This means that the Lord was giving them a prayer to repeat as well as a formula for prayer. He was giving them what they could say as well as how they could formulate their own prayers.

I do not think that we can improve on the Lord's method of teaching. The teacher who wants to succeed will, first of all, give beginners what they should say to the Lord as prayer. Take, for example, when you want to lead someone to the Lord, do you not sometimes say, "If you want to receive the Lord Jesus as your Lord and Saviour, repeat this prayer after me"? Then you have gone on to pray a prayer of repentance from sin and faith in the Lord Jesus

Christ and, by the time it was over, often the person has made the needed contact with God and is saved. Often, afterwards, I have gone ahead to lead the person to thank the Lord for his salvation, and to confess to the Lord the privilege of his new position, as well as tell the devil that his hold on the person is broken.

The person needs this helpful introduction, or else he might be ready but not know how to make the preliminary contact.

I was to confess that early in my Christian life I rebelled against written prayers that were repeated. There might have been reasons for my rebellion because of the abuse of these. I decided that I would teach young converts to pray from the word "go" in their own words and from their own hearts. I soon found that there were people who wanted to repent and be saved, whose background was such that they were totally at a loss as to what to say. I had to have them say what I was saying to God. I "plugged in" to the Father and prayed as if I were receiving Him for the first time and, as the people used my words, the Father saw beyond the words and imparted to them the power to become the sons of God. I have done this for an individual, for small groups and for crowds and, by God's grace, some have, thereby, touched divine life. I also found that I had to lead people in prayers of deliverance, healing, consecration and infilling with the Holy Spirit, and God has been glad to honour it. The other thing I have noticed is that when people have been told to pray on their own, they did not do so. They copied the person who was asking them to pray and prayed what he prayed!

The Lord taught the disciples what to say. He was correct. We have been doing the same and not realizing it and at the same time condemning those who use some forms of written prayers. This is not fair. It calls for repentance.

The important thing is that what is being said should come from the heart and lips and not from the lips only. It is possible to use the words of another person and let them flow from the heart and lips. We do it often when we quote the Scriptures in our praying to God and in our conflict with the Enemy, do we not? We use the Psalms as prayers and as songs without fearing that we are repeating someone else. Let us face this squarely. There is room to use the words and the thought forms of another to pray acceptably. My fear is that, because we are so anxious to make everyone independent in his praying, we are causing many people not to make progress. I realized that there were many believers who wanted to pray but did not know how to pray or what to pray about. So, instead of just asking people to pray for me, I sent them prayer topics which were the way I had prayed for the matter myself. This helped many people to understand my needs more clearly and to pray for them in the same direction in which I was praying. It helped them also to see areas in which they could pray for themselves. One brother told me, "When I receive your prayer topics I first pray them for myself as far as they are applicable to myself, which is often at depths, breadths and heights that through ignorance I could not have prayed for myself. It has made praying rich and interesting and I am seeing God answering my prayers more than I did in the past. Praise the Lord."

Fully convinced that it is not only necessary to stir up people to pray but also to help them to know what to pray about, we have written the next two books in this series. The books are, Practical Helps for Praying Believers, Volume One, How to Pray for Yourself; and Volume Two, How to Pray for Your Local Assembly. Below are three chapters from Volume One on the part, "Praying for Your Family." Pray through them and see if they help you to be more fulfilled as you pray for your mate. Praise the Lord!

PRAYING FOR A WIFE

1. Thanksgiving to the Lord for her salvation and for all the ways and all the areas of her life in which she has grown spiritually. The different ways and areas should be mentioned to the Lord

in detail.

2. Pray for her total deliverance from all sin. Bring to the Lord those areas in which she is still bound by sin. Name each sin to the Lord. Ask the Lord to open her eyes to see:
   a) that it is sin,
   b) to hate it,
   c) to desire deliverance,
   d) to seek deliverance,
   e) to repent,
   f) to be delivered,
   g) to remain delivered.
3. Pray for her total deliverance from the self-life. Expose to the Lord, all the ways in which the self-life is manifested in her life: self-justification, withdrawal, moods, harshness, indiscipline and so on. Ask the Lord to open her eyes to those things and that she should see them as manifestations of self, hate them, seek deliverance from the Lord, receive del verance from the Lord and remain delivered.
4. Pray that she should be delivered from laziness that is manifested in:
   a) too much sleep,
   b) procrastination,
   c) unaccomplished projects.
5. Pray that she should become a hardworking woman by applying herself to the diligent use of time by:
   a) working out a schedule for the week,
   b) working out a schedule for each day,
   c) abiding by the schedule as much as possible,
   d) giving accounts by the writing of all failures.

6. Pray that she should grow in the School of Prayer by:
   a) learning to contact God,
   b) learning to maintain the contact,
   c) learning to hear Him,
   d) learning to speak to Him,
   e) learning to commune with Him,
   f) learning to present requests,
   g) learning to receive answers,
   h) learning to enjoy His presence,
   i) learning to walk with Him after the prayer session.
7. Pray that she should grow in the School of Obedience by:
   a) learning to be totally consecrated daily, hourly, and every second,
   b) learning to hear God's voice,
   c) learning to believe that it is God speaking,
   d) making a radical commitment to obey,
   e) being meticulous in recording all that God has said,
   f) working out the way in which obedience is going to be manifested in each situation,
   g) rendering instantaneous obedience in all things to the Lord,
   h) putting aside all other commitments that were made before and that will stand in the way of obedience,
   i) asking and receiving from the Lord a spirit of rejoicing in obedience.
8. Pray that her commitment to the Word of God should be deep and radical and that she should commit herself to:
   a) read it (about ten chapters a day),
   b) study it,
   c) meditate on it,

d) memorize it,

e) obey it,

f) teach it to others.

9. Pray that her times of Dynamic Encounters with God (Quiet Time) should be:
   a) regular (each morning or at least six times a week),
   b) deep and thorough,
   c) times of meeting God and not just the analysis of His Word,
   d) times that give a sense of direction and purpose to the day,
   e) times that enable her to carry a sense of God's presence and glory into all of the day.
10. Pray that she should be deeply committed to the redemption of time and that:
   a) she should see time as one of the most precious gifts of God,
   b) she should see time as a perishable gift, that every minute not well used is lost for ever,
   c) she should see that she will give account on Judgment Day for the way she has used each second, minute, hour, day, week, month and year.
11. Pray that God's call on her life should become increasingly obvious; so that she should see clearly that one thing to which God has called her, Pray that if she has not yet received the goal God has for her life, she should seek it, find it and give all of herself to it. Pray that she should organise her life in such a way that her hourly, daily, weekly and monthly goals are all a real part of the one goal God has for her.
12. Pray that she should grow in Christian character. Make a list of the areas in which the fruit of the Spirit is underdeveloped in her life and bring each up to the Lord for rapid transformation.

Pray that she should hate these flaws and be totally determined to have all of them eliminated as soon as possible.

13. Pray that she should be delivered from all covetousness and love of the world and that this deliverance should be manifested by the following disappearing from her life:
    a) a spirit of comparison,
    b) love of vanity,
    c) love of what others have,
    d) dissatisfaction with what she has,
    e) a desire for worldly position and honours, promotions, appointments, diplomas, and so on,
    f) the lack of total satisfaction with what she has,
    g) a spirit of ingratitude and the tendency to keep things that are not really needed.
14. Pray that she should seek the Lord with her whole heart by going on regular:
    a) three-hour retreats,
    b) six-hour retreats,
    c) twelve-hour retreats,
    d) twenty-four-hour retreats,
    e) many day retreats and that her hunger for the Lord should be deep and insatiable. Pray that she should be fully satisfied in the Lord.
15. Pray that she should see the world for what it is: a judged system that will soon be removed, that her eyes should be fixed on heaven and that she should labour to invest everything there as soon as possible. Pray that she should live in hourly and daily expectation of the Lord and that her total person should be ready to meet Him in the air.

Thank the Lord for the time of prayer and believe Him for answers to all the requests you have made to Him.

DAILY PRAYING FOR A WIFE

1. Thank the Lord for her in a general way.
2.
   a) Thank the Lord for His goodness to her yesterday,
      - protection,
      - needs met,
      - and so on.

   b) Thank the Lord for the things that He enabled her to do yesterday.
3.
   a) Pray that the Lord should enable her to keep to the plan that she made the day before for today and that she should refuse to be distracted from it by any indiscipline.

   b) Pray that she should take time to plan the activities of tomorrow today and that she should write down the plans.
4. Pray for her time of meditation today. Ask the Lord to enable her to have it as the priority of priorities for the day. Pray that she should actually encounter the Lord during that time and that she should receive a touch of the Lord that will leave an impact on the whole day. Pray that she should obey the Lord in the things that He spoke to her about.
5. Pray for her prayer life:

   a) Ask the Lord to open her eyes to the priority of prayer.

   b) Protect it from attacks by the Enemy.

   c) Ask the Lord to enable her to keep to the planned prayer time.

   d) Lord, grant that she would enter into communion with

You in prayer.

e) Lord, show her what to ask in prayer.

f) Give her faith to believe You as she asks things of You.

g) Lord, enable her to mix her asking with thanksgiving.

h) Pray that she should be burdened to pray more.

6. Thank the Lord for her job and her professional life. Pray that she should work hard. Pray that the Lord should be exalted and glorified in her profession that day. Protect her job from attacks by the Enemy that day.
7. Pray for her relationship with her husband that day. Pray that:

a) she should love him,

b) she should submit to him and obey him,

c) she should be sensitive to his needs,

d) she should meet his needs,

e) she should be a good example to others,

f) her husband should be satisfied in her and with her,

g) he should encourage her,

h) she should be fulfilled as a wife.

8. Pray for her attitude to food! Pray that:

a) she should settle with God what she is to cook that day,

b) she should cook well without waste of time,

c) she should serve the food graciously and in Spirit-controlled quantities,

d) she and all she serves should not commit gluttony,

e) she should keep her kitchen clean for Your glory.

9. Pray for her attitude to money throughout the day. Pray that:

a) she should consecrate all the money to be used that day to the Lord,

b) she should seek God's will in the use of all money throughout the day,

c) she should record all expenses clearly,

d) she should be fully aware of the fact that she will soon appear before the Judgment Seat of Christ to give account of how each franc was used.

10. Pray for her attitude to visitors throughout the day. Pray that:

a) she should receive all visitors with joy and warmth and with prayer that God should guide and overrule in all that will transpire between her and the visitor,

b) God should give her a capacity to put each visitor at ease in her presence,

c) she should discern the needs of each and meet them,

d) she should be disciplined and honest with each visitor so that none stays more than is absolutely necessary for his needs to be met,

e) she should witness to the unbelieving visitors and reach out in a ministry of exhortation to the believing ones.

11. Pray that the Lord should strengthen her in the points of her great strength, which include:

a)

b)

c)

12. Pray that the Lord should reach out to her and help her to overcome her principal weaknesses which include the following:

a)

b)

c)

13. Pray that the Lord should prepare her to encounter the unexpected events of the day with joy and much self-control. Pray

that she should not become impatient or angry when things do not go the way she planned or the way she wants.

14.

a)Pray that she should be delivered from the following sins that plague many people in the household of God :

- moods,
- complaining,
- gossip,
- discouragement.

b) Pray that she should be given a genuine conviction of sin if she falls into any of these sins, so that she should repent, confess them, turn away from them, seek and receive pardon from God, and carry out the necessary restitution.

15. Pray for her physical health:

a) Protect it from every attack by the wicked one.

b) Ask the Lord to heal her of any and every disease that she may have.

c) Ask that she should not only know divine healing but that she should know the Lord Jesus as her perpetual health.

16. Pray that she should live the whole day in the Lord's presence, desiring and hastening the return of the Lord by:

a) her attitude in ministering to the Lord,

b) her attitude in ministering to the saints,

c) her attitude in ministering to those without Christ,

d) her attitude to the devil,

e) her attitude to the world,

f) her attitude to the flesh,

g) her attitude to the self in her.

17. Pray that she should put all that she has and all that she is into the day for the glory of the Lord; since that could be her last

day on Planet Earth. Pray that she should not hold back any good thing that she could do and should not postpone doing it.

18. Pray that she should live the whole day in the knowledge that she has the assurance of one of two possible appointments and either of them could be that day, namely:
    a) the sudden return of the Lord for His own,
    b) the sudden arrival of death.

DAILY PRAYING FOR A HUSBAND

1. Thank the Lord for him in a general way but for specific items.
2. Thank the Lord for His goodness to him yesterday:
    - protection,
    - needs met,
    - and so on.
3. Thank the Lord for the things that He enabled him to accomplish yesterday in the following domains:
    a) God's service,
    b) at his place of work,
    c) In the home.
4.
    a) Pray that the Lord should enable him to plan every day in advance and that the plans should be God-directed.
    b) Pray that he should plan the day of tomorrow today and that there should be a clear goal to be accomplished.
    c) Pray that he should keep to the plan for today and labour to ensure that the goal set for today is attained.
    d) Pray that he should write down the plans and in the evening have the courage to face them for evaluation.
5. Pray for his time of meditation:

a) that he should be disciplined so as to keep to the scheduled time,
b) that he should hunger to meet God,
c) that he should actually meet God and not just analyse and apply the Word,
d) that he should receive a touch of the Lord that will be his strength for the day,
e) that he would obey the Lord in the things that He spoke to him about.

6. Pray for his prayer life, that:
   a) his eyes should be opened increasingly to the priority of prayer,
   b) he should make prayer his priority,
   c) his prayer times previously fixed should be respected,
   d) his prayer times should be protected from the attacks of the wicked one,
   e) he should enter into communion with God in prayer,
   f) he should ask and receive from the Lord what to ask in prayer,
   g) he should be given faith to believe God as he asks in prayer,
   h) he should listen to God during his time of prayer,
   i) God should speak to him as he prays; so that it should be a dialogue and not a monologue,
   j) he should fulfil his office as the priest of the home by interceding for his wife, each of his children and any other members of his household,
   k) he should know how to mingle his asking with thanksgiving to the Lord,
   l) he should be enabled to fulfil part of his office as the pro-

phet of the home by leading in teaching the Word during family devotion in the morning,

m) he should be burdened to pray more.

7. Pray for his job and professional life in the following way:
   a) Thank the Lord for his job and all the income he has earned in the past.
   b) Thank the Lord for his previous professional performance. Be very specific.
   c) Pray that the Lord should enable him to put on and maintain the attitude of a servant at his place of work.
   d) Pray that he should be loyal to his boss, obedient and respectful to all his seniors and kind to his juniors.
   e) Pray that he should work very hard, so that the Lord may be glorified in his professional life.
   f) Pray that he should not do Christian work instead of his professional work at his place of work, so that his salary should be justifiably earned.
   g) Pray that the Lord should enable him to make a distinct professional contribution.
   h) Pray that as the Lord opens the door, he should witness to his colleagues and win them for Christ.
   i) Pray that he should not be persecuted, unless the Lord has designed it to be so, because of his faith.
   j) Pray that he should be promoted when he deserves promotion but that he should not be moved by elevations in the world.
   k) Pray that he should have professional fulfilment at his job.
8. Pray for his relationship with his wife, that:
   a) he should love and cherish her increasingly,
   b) he should honour, encourage, and appreciate instead of depreciating her,

c) he should have the courage to correct her in love,

d) he should be gentle, kind and considerate to her in all things,

e) he should be faithful to her in thought, word and deed as unto the Lord,

f) he should be protected from the attractions of other women,

g) he should give a helping hand joyfully with house work as the need may be,

h) he should pray for her daily and also pray with her daily, even if it is just for a few minutes,

i) his wife should find fulfilment in him and blossom as a woman,

j) he should bear with her faults and weaknesses and help her to overcome them.

9. Pray for him as a father, that:

a) he should love each child deeply,

b) he should encourage each child by word, letter or gift as the need may be,

c) he should notice the weaknesses of each child and labour to have them taken away by prayer and practical application,

d) he should pray for each child in a specific manner,

e) he should apply Spirit-controlled discipline to the children where necessary,

f) he should be sensitive to the needs of each child and labour to meet them,

g) he should thank the Lord for each child and consider it a privilege to be his/her father,

h) he should set a good example in everything before the children,

i) the children should love and obey him in all things,

j) the children should be at home with him so that they can share their problems and needs freely with him,

k) he should be fulfilled as a father.

10. Pray for his attitude to money throughout the day, that:

a) he should consecrate all the money he is to use to the Lord,

b) he should seek the Lord's will about every franc before use,

c) he should be transparent to his wife about all monetary matters,

d) he should record all income and expenditures,

e) he should be fully aware that he may be called up by the Lord that day to give an account of his financial stewards-hip.

11. Pray for his ministry to the Lord, the Lord's people and the lost, that:

a) he should become a minister to the Lord by being a true worshipper who worships the Lord in Spirit and in truth and that he should seek to know the Lord's needs and to minister to Him according to those needs,

b) he should carry his ministry to God, the saints and the lost on his heart and that it will weigh on him,

c) he should relentlessly pursue the goals that he received from the Lord for his ministry,

d) he should pursue the goal that he set for that day and do all to accomplish it,

e) he should make prayer the priority of his ministry to God, the saints and the lost,

f) he should be delivered from the sins of comparison, pride and jealousy and should labour to satisfy the Lord alone,

g) he should sacrificially put in his all: time, money and energy into the call of God on his life.

12. Pray for his points of strength, which are:
    a)
    b)
    c))
    and so on.

    That:
    - the Lord should bless him more and more,
    - the Lord should enable him to further develop in these areas,
    - the Lord should deliver him from the fatal sin of pride.
13. Pray for his points of weakness, which include:
    a)
    b)
    c)
    and so on.

    That the Lord should:
    - open his eyes to see them,
    - enable him to accept himself with his weaknesses and not develop an inferiority complex,
    - enable him to humble himself before the Lord, desiring and requesting to be delivered,
    - enable him to co-operate with Him for his deliverance, so that his weaknesses can be taken away.
14. Pray that the Lord should deliver him from the following sins that plague many men:
    a) lust,
    b) impatience,
    c) covetousness,
    d) Discouragement.
15. Pray that he should see the gravity of each of these sins before

the Lord.

- Pray that he should have an intimate relationship with the Holy Spirit; so that he should be deeply convicted, should he fall into any.
- Pray that when convicted he should repent immediately and genuinely and seek the Lord's forgiveness and restoration.
- Pray that he should be filled with the Holy Spirit daily; so that he should know a continuous walk in purity.

16. Pray for his physical health that he should be delivered from all the attacks of the Enemy through:

    a) his ministry to the Lord,

    b) his ministry to the saints,

    c) his ministry to the lost,

    d) his attitude to Satan,

    e) his attitude to a judged and condemned world;

    f) his attitude to the flesh,

    g) his attitude to the self-life in him.

17. Praise the Lord for having enabled you to pray for him.

    Amen.

17

JESUS TAUGHT THEM SPIRITUAL CONTACT

The Lord Jesus in teaching the disciples on how to pray ensured that the first lesson was on spiritual contact. He taught this by saying to them, "When you pray, say: Our Father in heaven."

What was the significance of this? I think there are two main points. The first is contact and the second is humility. The disciple is praying to a Father. He is not praying to a force. He is not praying to an idea. He is not praying to the wind. If he is praying to a Father, then he has to ensure that there is communion between him and the Father. Which child would want to speak to his father and not labour to ensure that he first drew the father's attention, was rightly related to his father and that his father was disposed to listen to him?

Many believers do not pray. They just make noise and rattle things and go away. They come back and go through the same ritual and never make any progress. They wonder why they are not making progress in the knowledge of God. They wonder why they are not making progress in prayer. The truth is that they cannot make progress in prayer. They can also not make progress in the knowledge and love of God, because they are not plugged into God. Can an electric kettle which is not plugged in to the source of electricity wonder why the water in it is not getting hot? The truth is that it cannot get hot because it is out of contact. I could remain in that condition for years and never get anywhere. The question may arise in some heart, "How can I get in touch? How can I 'plug in' to the Father so that I will talk to Him and hear Him talk to me?"

To answer that question we need to define prayer. Prayer is not only talking to God; prayer is, first of all, listening to God. It is, secondly, hearing God and it is, thirdly, talking to God.

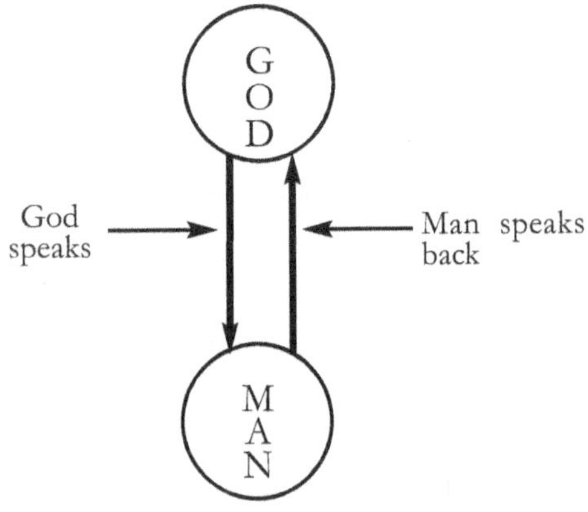

What prayer is.

God should be allowed to take the initiative. However, even if the believer is to take the initiative, he should ensure that God is listening to him; so that God will talk back or answer him.

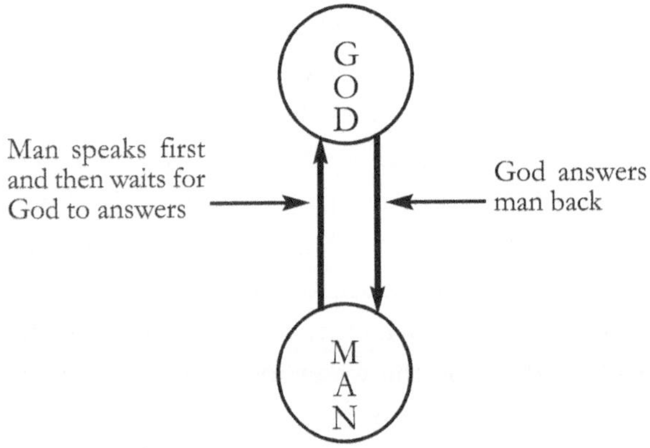

What prayer is.

HOW TO PLUG IN TO GOD

There will be times of emergency when the child will not wait to plug in to God normally. He will have to take for granted that the Father is listening. Such emergencies do occur in practical human life. Take, for example, that a child is being chased by thieves. He will not go quietly to the father and ask for protection. He will cry out from a distance, "Daddy, Daddy, help me for I am in trouble." The father will hear and run to his rescue. The child's approach to the father was unconventional and the father responded. If, on the other hand, there is no emergency and the son, instead of quietly walking to the father and waiting in his presence until he is called upon to speak, just rushes into his presence and begins to rattle one thing after another, this will be considered to be rudeness and he may be allowed to go away unattended to.

When a believer wants to pray, he should, first of all, ask himself some questions, which will include :

1. Am I in the right condition to go into God's presence?
2. Is there any unconfessed sin in my life?
3. Have I done the work that was assigned to me the last time that I was in His presence?

The asking of these questions may lead to confessing and forsaking obvious sins. It may also lead to carrying out some acts of obedience without which future fellowship with God may be greatly impaired. ANYONE WHO THINKS THAT HE CAN REPEATEDLY RECEIVE INSTRUCTIONS FROM GOD AND DISOBEY THEM, AND YET COME TO HIM FOR MORE FELLOWSHIP AND FURTHER INSTRUCTIONS, IS MISTAKEN. Normally, God demands obedience of past instructions before He can give further ones. Anyone who thinks that He can disobey what God asked him to do previously, yet come to Him to ask that his current needs be met, is taking God's grace in vain. God may answer him for some more time, but the relationship will deteriorate;

so that the person will obtain less and less from God and have decreasing communion and clarity in prayer.

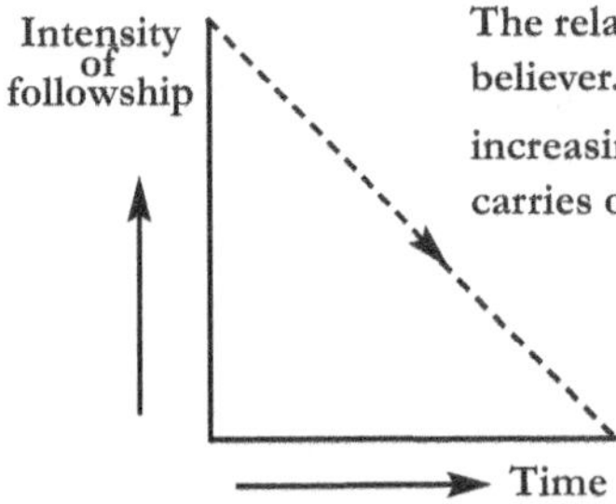

The relation between God and the desobedient believer. There is decreasing fellowship with increasing time until the believer repents and carries out restitution.

The believer who has not carried out previous instructions or who finds that he has sinned should come to the Lord and say, "Father, I have sinned. My sin is I repent of it and will not go that way again. Please forgive me for breaking Your law and grant that I should be able to fellowship with You again." The Lord will forgive such a one and he can continue to communicate with Him.

When a believer comes before God, having examined himself and seen that there is no barrier between him and the eternal Father, he should wait before the Lord quietly. Two things will happen. There may be sin in his life which he could not see on his own but now that he has come into God's presence, everything is exposed by the glory of His presence. Seeing things then as they are, that believer will repent, confess the sin and ask to be forgiven and restored to fellowship with the Lord. The Lord will forgive him and restore him, and then he can go on in the presence of the Lord.

The believer who, in the presence of God does not see anything in his life that could cause a barrier, should say to the Lord, "Father, I do not want to deceive myself. According to the way I see things, there is no sin that I know of in my life that I have committed but not repented of. You know me better than I know myself and you see what I do not see. If I have committed some sin and forgotten about it, if I committed it but did not realize that it was sin, I plead in the name of the Lord Jesus that You should have mercy on me and show me the sin; so that I may confess and forsake it." Such a one should wait quietly before the Lord in silence. If there is something wrong, the Lord will show him, but if nothing is wrong, he will find that he becomes increasingly peaceful in the presence of the Lord and also feels quite at home. He may find that being silent before God is increasingly interesting and the sense of fear is being replaced by a real sense of liberty. The person has "plugged in." Communion has indeed been established. Communication can now start.

One of two things would happen at this point. The believer could take the initiative and begin to worship and praise the Lord, confessing the Lord's goodness and giving Him thanks for past faithfulness, or he could continue to wait in silence before the Lord. If he chooses to continue to wait in silence before the Lord, the Lord will take the initiative to begin the conversation, and this is wonderful. It could be that after waiting for some time the communion is maintained and he takes the initiative to say, "Lord, Your servant is waiting before You, anxious to hear You speak to him. Lord, speak; for Your servant heareth." After that the Lord may begin to speak or the waiting believer may have the liberty to begin to speak.

There are mature believers who come into God's presence and, after contact has been established, prefer to wait before the Lord rather than initiate anything. They have understood that true praying starts in the heart of God. They have also come to know that it is better to wait in God's presence in silence and just enjoy His presence than to talk. They know a level of communion with God that is beyond words, and so they prefer not to say a thing. They are just enraptured by the Lord, so overwhelmed by His goodness that they dare not "spoil" the beauty and wonder of it with words, be they known, unknown or groans. This is the lot of mature believers and if immature believers merely want to imitate this waiting before the Lord in silence, they will either become restless or they will fall asleep. Such should then know that they are at the level where they may need to take the initiative and talk to the Lord after contact has been established.

When contact has been established, and throughout the time of prayer, the believer must remember that he is before the Father who is in heaven. He should, consequently, feel free before his Father. He should, on the other hand, be full of awe because his Father is in heaven and he is on earth and even the dust on the Father's feet outweighs him utterly. This knowledge, should help him to be humble. It should determine what he says to God and how he says it; for there is always a difference in content and manner of talking that depends on whether one is talking to a superior, an equal or an inferior; there can be no room for anyone shouting at God; for do normal people shout at their superiors? Certainly not. Amen.

18

JESUS TAUGHT THEM BY HIS OWN LIFE THAT WHAT A PERSON IS, IS CRITICALLY IMPORTANT TO THE IMPACT THAT HIS PRAYERS WILL PRODUCE

"The Lord Jesus taught, "*For everyone who asks receives, and he who seeks finds, and to him who knocks it will be opened*" (Luke 11:10).

This being a statement of the Lord Jesus, it must be true. Does it, however, mean that any believer can ask for anything and it will be given him? Does it mean hat whatever a person seeks he will find? Does it mean that whatever any person knocks for and regardless of what door he knocks it will be opened to him? I do not think so. What a person is, is critically important in everything. It is even more important in prayer.

The principle of what a person is and its impact on what he does works as follows :

a) In prayer : Two people of varying degrees of consecration who, nevertheless, pray over the same issue, will produce varying impact.

b) In giving : Two people of varying consecration who give the same.

Percentage of their income to the Lord will produce different degrees of impact with their gifts.

The impact of the gifts of the one who is more consecrated will be greater on his life, ministry, the heart of God and others.

c) In Bible reading : Two people, one consecrated and the other unconsecrated, even if they have the same basic education, were converted at the same time and have received the same teaching will, on reading the Word, receive different truths and at different depths. This will be in proportion to their level of consecration.

d) In evangelism : Evangelists of varying consecration will preach the Gospel and it will produce converts of varying commitments to the Lord.

e) In teaching : Bible teachers of varying consecration will produce varying impact with their teaching of the same doctrine.

f) In everything : What a man is will influence what he does in every area of his life. No one can run away from this.

Because everyone who asks receives, and everyone who seeks finds and everyone who knocks has it opened for him, we will now show that there are varying degrees of receiving for asking, finding for seeking and its being opened for knocking.

This can be tied to the fact that a man's asking is fundamentally related to what he is. The same goes for his seeking and knocking. No one can ask, seek and knock beyond the level at which he knows God, has obeyed God and is separated unto God. A man may wish for great things and use big words in prayer, but when all gets before God, it takes the level of what the person is before God.

This being the case, the most important thing then is not that a person prays. The most important thing is that a person should be what God meant him to be: totally consecrated, totally separated from sin, totally separated from the love of the world, totally separated from the love of self, and so on. Then, when he prays, his praying will produce the results that God intended them to produce. The sad thing is that there are many believers who are praying but, because of something wrong in their hearts, they are not able to produce the impact that God intended them to produce. They are sub-normal, pray sub-normal prayers and make sub-normal impact.

53 The entirely consecrated believer who knocks unceasingly.
50 The entirely consecrated believer who knocks and knocks.
46 The entirely consecrated believer who knocks.
43 The entirely consecrated believer who seeks and seeks.
41 The consecrated believer who seeks.
39 The entirely consecrated believer who asks and asks.
38 The entirely consecrated believer who asks.
36 The entirely consecrated believer.
35
34
32 The partially consecrated believer who knocks and knocks.
31 The partially consecrated believer who knocks.
30 The partially consecrated believer who seeks and seeks.
29 The partially consecrated believer who seeks.
28 The partially consecrated believer who asks and asks.
27 The partially consecrated believer who asks.
26 The partially consecrated believer who does not ask.
25
24 The unconsecrated believer who knocks and knocks.

23 The unconsecrated believer who knocks.

22 The unconsecrated believer who seeks and seeks.

21 The unconsecrated believer who seeks.

20 The unconsecrated believer who asks and asks.

19 The unconsecrated believer who asks.

18 All believers, even if they are totally unconsecrated.

17

16

15

14 Those unbelievers who respond to the light that they have received, live according to it and knock and knock.

13 Those unbelievers who respond to the light that they have received, live according to it and knock.

12 Those unbelievers who respond to the light that they have received, live according to it and seek and seek.

11 Those unbelievers who respond to the light that they have received, live according to it and seek.

10 Those unbelievers who respond to the light that they have received, live according to it and ask and ask.

9 Those unbelievers who respond to the light that they have received, live according to it and ask.

8 Those unbelievers who repent and live according to the light they have received but do not ask.

7 Those wicked unbelievers who knock and knock.

6 Those wicked unbelievers who

5 Those wicked unbelievers who

4 Those wicked unbelievers who

3 Those wicked unbelievers who

2 Those wicked unbelievers who

1 All unbelievers who receive from the Lord, even if they are most wicked. Each intersection could be a level, that is, the gap can be wider than is actually represented.

Let us look at a wordly example:

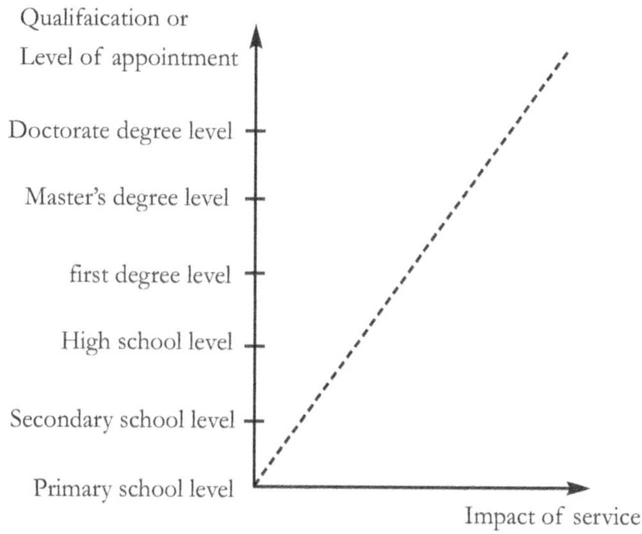

The Impact of Qualification or Appointment on Service

THE IMPACT OF QUALIFICATION OR APPOINTMENT ON SERVICE

The impact of the work of someone who has a doctorate degree is greater than someone who has a master's degree and so forth. His one hour of work is of greater consequence. The same is obvious when the service of a graduate and someone with a High School diploma is concerned.

If a Head of State works in his office for one hour, the consequence of that one-hour service on the nation may be greater than the consequence of the work of a lifetime of a cleaner or messenger. Impact is dependent on the level of appointment.

In the spiritual realm the impact of a person's praying is proportional to what the person's level of consecration is, and for how long he prays.

If a sin-loving believer asks, he will receive something of the Lord. If, on the other hand, he asks and asks, he will receive more from the Lord at his level. If he asks and asks, seeks and seeks and knocks and knocks, he will receive increasingly from the Lord and have increasing impact, but the impact will always be within the level that is possible for him. There are levels of asking, seeking and knocking which are totally barred to the unconsecrated believer.

If an entirely consecrated believer prays for one hour, the impact of that one hour of prayer is far more than the impact of one month or one year of the praying of a sin-loving believer! You can understand this if you consider the fact that the monthly salary of someone with a doctorate degree may be more than the annual salary of someone who has, say, the First School Leaving Certificate. So every hour of prayer by a consecrated believer is a major issue, whereas the days, weeks and even years of the praying of one who is unconsecrated or partially consecrated, amount to little.

We sometimes say that someone prays for three, four, six or eight hours a day. That may indicate a fair level of discipline. However, it is possible to pray for many hours while having a controversy with God. It is possible to pray for ten hours a day for six months while having some secret sin that is not confessed and forsaken. Such long periods of praying by partially consecrated believers make some contribution, but they are nothing compared to the same amount of time put in by a believer who is entirely consecrated.

Are you boasting about the number of hours that you put into prayer, whereas they are the hours of a divided heart that have very little value before God?

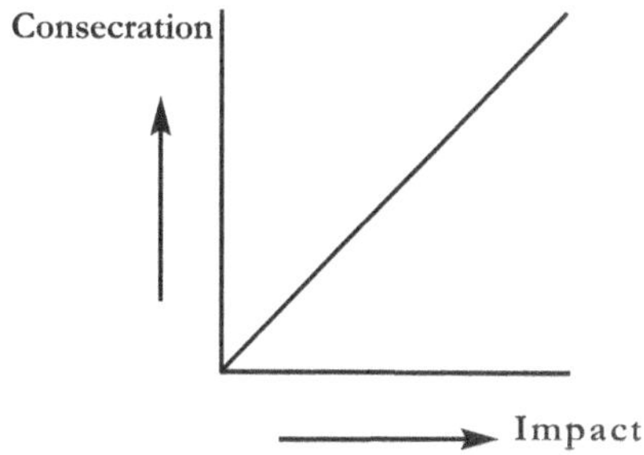

The more consecrated make greater impact with their praying. The less consecrated make less impact with their praying.

The impact is also proportional to the time invested in praying. We illustrate this as follows: Two believers of the same degree of consecration, one who prays for one hour daily and the other for three hours daily will manifest different degrees of impact. Their praying will influence their lives and all else in proportion to the time put in. That is why the person who prays once or twice and the person who prays and prays over the same issue will have varying results.

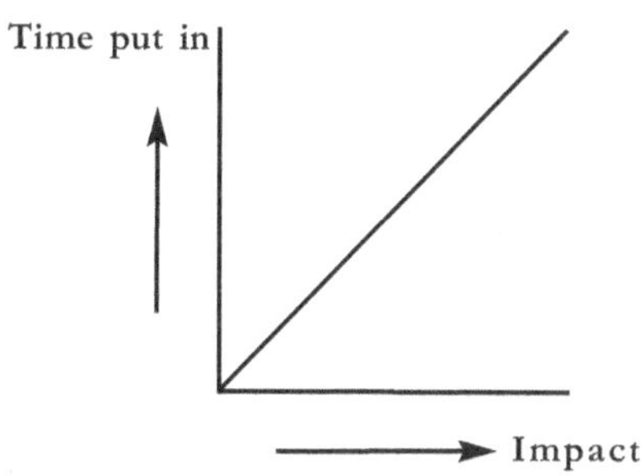

The Relationship between the Time put into Praying and the Impact of the Praying

The impact is also proportional to the intensity of praying. Someone can pray leisurely for one hour and another person prays violently for one hour. It is obvious that the two people will not produce the same results. The person who is more intense, more desperate and more violent will certainly accomplish more with his one hour than his leisurely brother with his.

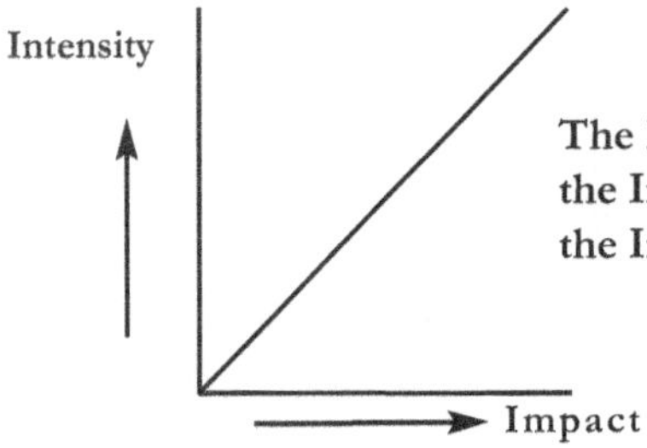

The Relationship between the Intensity of Praying and the Impact of the Praying

Do you see then that while one believer is totally involved, pouring all of himself to God in prayer and sweating, another may be there comfortably saying a few words and sparing himself?

The impact is also proportional to the number of people praying. If one consecrated believer prays, there is impact. If ten consecrated believers pray, there is greater impact. If one hundred, one thousand, one million believers pray, the impact is proportional to the number of people praying. Whether the impact is simple, arithmetic or geometric, is not ours to know. We know from Scripture that it is at least simply proportional.

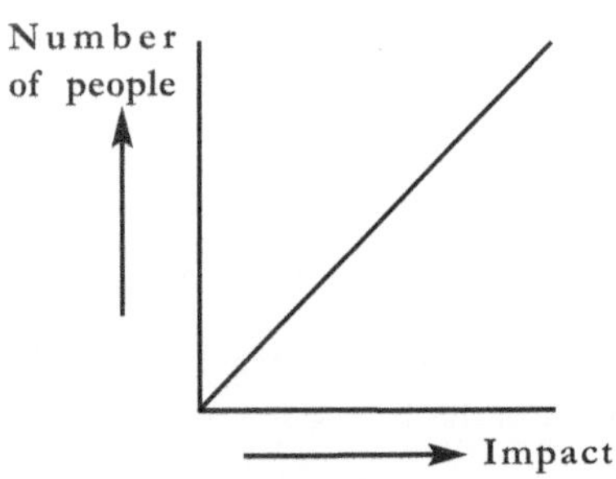

The Relationship between the Number of people Praying on a certain Issue and the Impact

The impact is also proportional to knowledge of facts. A consecrated believer can have clear knowledge of the facts of a situation in detail. He can also have a clear knowledge of what God wants and, on the basis of this knowledge, prays. Such praying will produce great impact. On the other hand, a consecrated believer can have only vague ideas about a situation and only vague ideas as to what God wants. He may still pray, but the impact will be relatively lower than that produced by the believer who prays according to knowledge. Take, for example, two consecrated believers who are praying about a journey to be effected by a brother. One knows the dates, the flights, the countries, the objective of the journey, and so on, while the other one only knows that the brother is going on a journey. Both cannot pray with the same intensity and, consequently, cannot produce the same impact.

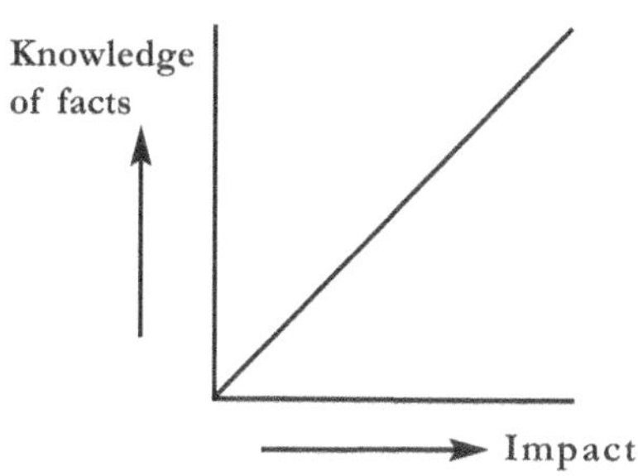

The Relationship between the Knowledge of Facts and the Impact

Impact is also proportional to the extent to which the praying person has been delivered from the love of the world.

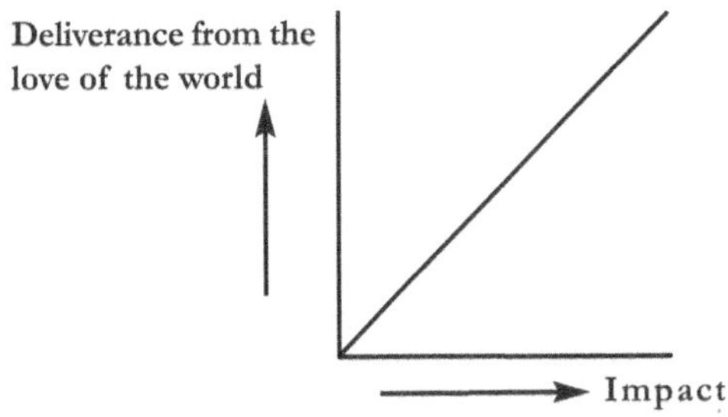

The Relationship between the Extent of Deliverance from the Love of the World and the Impact in Praying

The one who has known deeper deliverance from the love of the world will make greater impact in prayer than the one who, while still loving the world and the things in the world, nevertheless, prays.

Impact is also proportional to the extent to which the praying person has been delivered from the self-life.

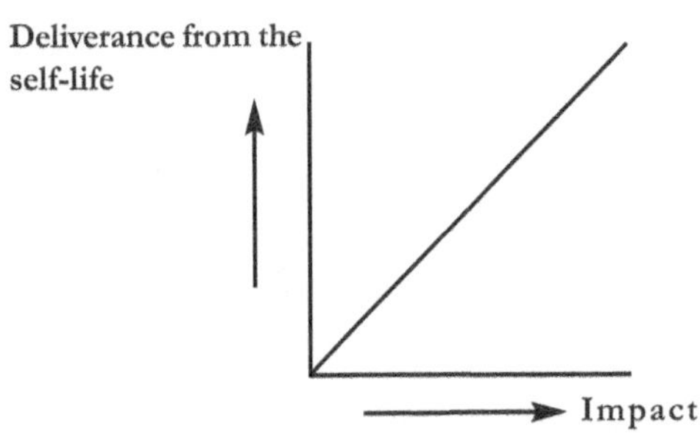

The Relationship between the Extent of Deliverance from the Self-Life and Impact in Praying

Again, it is obvious that the one who yields his self-life to ruthless dealings by the cross, doing nothing to preserve the self and the self-life, will make greater impact before God by his praying than another person who, while praying, has, through protection of the self, reduced the effective work of the cross in bringing his self-life to an end.

Impact is also proportional to the faith of the praying person.

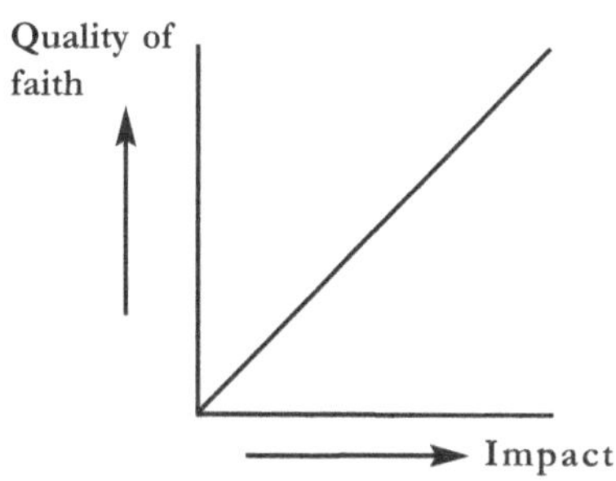

The Relationship between the Quality of Faith of the Praying Person and the Impact produced by His Praying

THE LORD JESUS WAS WHAT THE FATHER WANTED HIM TO BE

We have seen that what a person is, is critically important to the impact of his prayer life. There are people who seem to pray and pray, but their praying produces little impact on their lives, on the lives of others, on the Kingdom of God and on the kingdom of the evil one. Such people have a deep-seated problem somewhere in their lives.

The Lord Jesus was different. His life produced a lot of impact. When he prayed, things happened. What was His secret? The secret lay in :

1. His sinless life. He could challenge His opponents with, "*Which of you convicts me of sin?*" (John 8:46). None answered, for there was no sin in Him. He said, "*The prince of this world is coming, and he has nothing in Me*" (John 14:30, NKJV). The

testimony of the Bible is that He was tempted in every respect as we are, yet without sin (Hebrews 4:15).

2. His consecration was total. He held nothing back.
3. He was totally delivered of Himself. The self-life of the Lord Jesus was not evil, yet even that was put away completely. The Bible says that He emptied Himself, and humbled Himself (Philippians 2:7-8).

Because Jesus was what His Father wanted Him to be, His prayer life produced far-reaching impact.

We must labour to be what the Father expects us to be in motive, thought, word and deed. Then we must pray as the Father expects us to pray and then our prayers will produce the impact that God ordained for them to produce. Glory be to His holy name! Amen.

19

JESUS TAUGHT THEM THAT THE FIRST PRIORITY IN PRAYER IS TO PRAY THAT GOD'S NAME BE HALLOWED

Many people consider that God instituted prayer to meet the needs of man. This is not actually so. Prayer was instituted so that, as it is executed His way, the needs of God might be met. Of course, He also intended that the one who laboured to see the needs of God met would in the very process have his deepest need met and then his secondary needs met. We can say then that prayer was instituted to meet the needs of God and the needs of man; to meet the deepest need of God and the deepest need of man.

The thought that God has needs may frighten and shock some, but this is actually true. Although God is eternally Self-sufficient, He, in His sovereignty, decided to create a need in Himself which man could satisfy. He intended that the supreme purpose of man would be the satisfaction of this need. He intended that, as man satisfied this need, his own deepest need would be met.

We then ask, "What is the greatest need of God?" We reply that the greatest need of God is that His holiness be proclaimed. This is seen in the fact that so often we see the angels proclaiming it. For example, the Bible says, "*Above him stood the Seraphim, each had six wings: with two he covered his face, and with two he covered his feet, and with two he flew.And one called to another and said, 'Holy, holy, holy is the Lord of hosts; the whole earth is full of his glory'* "

(Isaiah 6:2-3).

"*And the four living creatures, each of them with six wings, are full of eyes all round and within, and day and night they never cease to sing, 'Holy, holy, holy is the Lord God Almighty, who was and is and is to come*' " (Revelation 4:8). The angel of water said, "*Just art thou in these thy judgments, thou who art and wast, O Holy One*" (Revelation 16:5).

There are many aspects of the person of God revealed to us in the Bible. The one that stands out above all the others is His holiness. Let us look at a few verses:

1. "*Say to all the congregation of the people of Israel, You shall be holy; for I the Lord your God am holy*" (Leviticus 19:2).
2. "*You shall be holy to me; for I the Lord am holy, and have separated you from the peoples, that you should be mine*" (Leviticus 20:26).
3. "*There is none holy like the Lord*" (1 Samuel 2:2).
4. "*Then the men of Bethshemesh said, 'Who is able to stand before the Lord, this holy God?*' " (1 Samuel 6:20).
5. "*Yet thou art holy, enthroned on the praises of Israel*" (Psalm 22:3).
6. "*Thus said the Lord God, the Holy One of Israel*" (Isaiah 30:15).

If the holiness of God is the most important thing, the priority attribute of God, then those who want to meet God's priority need would have to give themselves to praising and worshipping Him for His holiness; and labouring to ensure that that holiness is manifested in their lives and in the lives of others.

The greatest purpose and the greatest need of man, then, are to know, experience, praise, worship, and adore the holiness of God. He is to manifest the holiness of God in his life and, thirdly, he is to manifest the holiness of God in the world. God's ultimate purpose in creation is to have a people who praise and worship Him for His holiness and manifest His holiness.

This being the case, the first priority in prayer is to praise and bless God for His holiness, live in His presence and so put on His holiness, and then pray that people should behold His holiness and be holy themselves, and in turn pray that others be holy, and so on.

If this is the priority in prayer, then we have to acknowledge that most believers have missed it. Jesus, however, did not miss it. He taught on prayer and, as was and is normal of Him, He put things in their order of importance.

In that order, prayer is centred on God. It is :

- Hallowed be Thy name,
- Thy Kingdom come,
- Thy will be done.

It is not, "God, do this for me," or "God, give me this or that." Man is put aside completely. Oh that God would teach us this, that the very essence of prayer is the hallowing of God's name, the coming of God's Kingdom and the doing of God's will.

It is also important to note that of the three "Thy's" the first is not His will or His kingdom but His holiness.

We may illustrate this by saying that the holiness of God is at the very heart of God and then comes His Kingdom and, thirdly, His will.

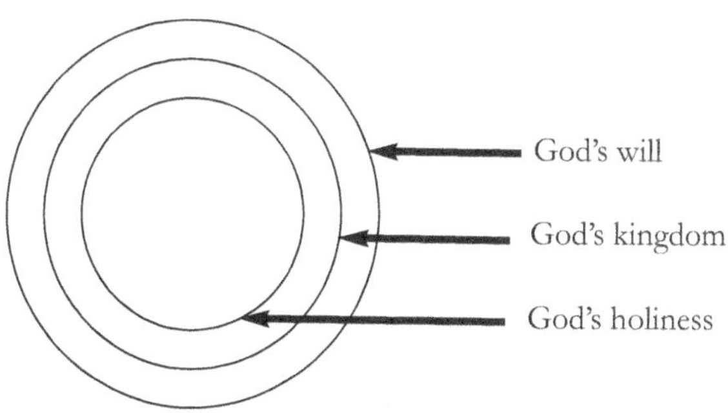

The Relationship between God's Holiness, Kingdom and Will

THE RELATIONSHIP BETWEEN GOD'S HOLINESS, KINGDOM AND WILL

God is first preoccupied with His holiness, and then with His kingdom, and lastly, with His will. Those who are preoccupied with men have missed it all. Those who are preoccupied with His will are preoccupied at a tertiary level. We must become preoccupied with His holiness.

The question is, how are we to be preoccupied with His holiness? To be preoccupied with His holiness, we, first of all, need to be decentralized of self. The one who is not delivered from self will, first of all, think about his needs and, secondarily, about the needs of man and only thirdly, about the needs of God. When he comes to the needs of God, he will put God's will first, God's Kingdom next and God's holiness last. Let us illustrate it this way :

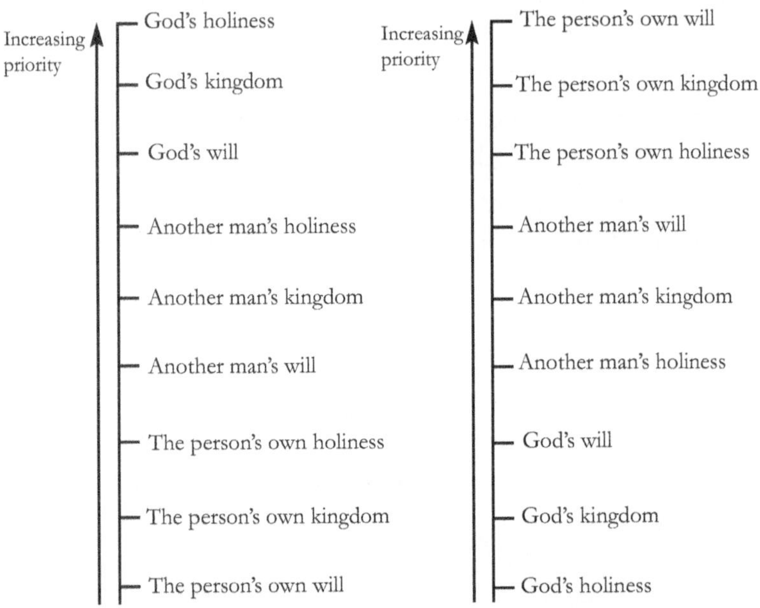

I confess that for many years as a believer I did not see the priorities of prayer the way the Lord saw them and demanded that I see them. How blind I have been, even though I have read the

Word many times!

I agree with God and His Word.

I agree that priority number one is for me to hallow God's name be lost in praising Him for His holiness. If I do this, I will be doing the first thing that God expects from me in prayer. In doing it, I will find deepest fulfilment for myself; for I was created to worship Him.

The next thing is that I will pray that others be taken up with the worship of the Lord for His holiness. I will then pray that my life should be holy so that I can enter freely into the presence of the God of holiness. I will also pray that the Lord should render the lives of other believers holy; so that they, too, will worship the Lord of all holiness in holiness. I will pray that the Lord should reveal His holiness to those without Christ, so that they, too, should come to the Lord and hallow His name.

It should finally be understood that the hallowing of God's name should, in the final analysis, become a way of life. That is what God meant it to be. His desire is that I should be so possessed by God and so taken up with His holiness that my motives, thoughts, words and acts will be all holy. In that way, all of my life will be a prayer, "Lord, hallowed be Thy name."

THE SCHOOL OF PRAYER; THE SCHOOL OF HOLINESS

If prayer is really an activity of holy people, then those who want to enter into The School of Prayer should first enrol with Christ in The School of Holiness. The Lord will teach them to be holy and then teach them how holy people pray. They will then praise, live and serve the Lord in holiness. In that way they shall be blessed.

"Lord God, I pray that You should enrol me in the Lord Jesus' School of Holiness and enable me to make rapid progress; so that my prayer life will be centred on Your holiness and thus bring glory to Your all-blessed name. Amen.

20

JESUS TAUGHT THEM THAT THE SECOND PRIORITY IN PRAYER IS TO PRAY THAT GOD'S KINGDOM SHOULD COME

As we saw in the preceding chapter, prayer was not instituted by the Lord to meet the needs of man. It was instituted to meet the needs of God. In prayer, the first step is the revelation of God's need to a waiting person who then prays it back to God for execution. We also said that the priority need of God was that His name be hallowed. He wants His holiness to be confessed. He also wants His holiness to be confessed by life, that is, He wants holiness to be confessed with lips and by life. It is when the Lord finds people who are fit to confess His holiness with lips and by life that He gets interested in people moving on to the next thing, which is His Kingdom. GOD HAS ORDAINED THAT ONLY THOSE WHO ARE CAUGHT UP WITH HIS HOLINESS, CONFESSING IT WITH LIPS AND BY LIFE, SHOULD BE INVOLVED WITH HIS KINGDOM. THOSE WHO DO NOT KNOW GOD'S HOLINESS AS A REALITY IN THEIR LIVES, HAVE NOTHING TO OFFER TO HIS KINGDOM. IN FACT, ALL THEIR ATTEMPTS TO ADVANCE THE KDINGDOM CAN ONLY HINDER IT.

The Lord then taught that His second priority need is His kingdom. That is, the second priority in prayer should be centred on the labour to have His kingdom come.

There are actually three kingdoms. There is the kingdom of God. There is also the kingdom of man and thirdly there is the kingdom of the wicked one. In order that the Kingdom of God might come, the kingdoms of man and Satan must give way.

To pray that the Kingdom of God should come is first to pray that your own kingdom should come to naught. None who protects his personal

interest,

inclinations,

tastes,

likes,

dislikes,

and so on,

can be caught up with prayer that the Kingdom of God should come, for the Kingdom of God will war against his personal kingdom. In fact, those who worship the self in them are of little consequence to God. The first battle is for the overthrow of the god "self." When that god is overthrown, the believer will unite himself fully with the Lord for the overthrow of Satan.

The Lord Jesus had no corrupt self to fight against. He, therefore, united Himself with the Father for the overthrow of Satan. He had no personal kingdom to build or to protect. He, therefore, gave Himself to co-operate with God for the overthrow of the kingdom of Satan.

The second priority in prayer then must begin with supplication that one's kingdom be brought to naught. Those who want to so pray must be resolute with God. They must plead that He should not allow any hiding place for self in them. They must pray, saying, "Lord, put an end to the 'self' in me and the 'self'-life in me at all costs." They must not only pray. They must watch out for any manifestations of the self-life and confess these to the Lord, as well as consign them to death on the cross. By such a rigorous application of themselves in a sustained manner in prayer and in action, they will overthrow self. With self overthrown, they will then actively unite themselves with the Father and by prayer and action, bring the kingdom of Satan to naught. IT REQUIRES THE COMBINED EFFORT IN PRAYER AND IN ANY OTHER WAY, BETWEEN LIBERATED MAN AND GOD, TO OVERTHROW THE KINGDOM OF SATAN.

When the kingdom of Satan is overthrown, no one should take for granted that God's Kingdom will just spontaneously be established. The one who has brought the kingdom of Satan to an end in his life must invite and beg the Lord to move in in majesty and power. The one who has brought the kingdom of Satan to an end in his family, village, town, nation, must invite the Lord to move in in majestic splendour. When thus invited, the Lord will come in and, as the Lord comes in, His kingdom will come in as well.

Of course, the ousted self and ousted Satan have to be kept away by vigilant prayer. Or, more accurately, the Lord and His Kingdom must be brought in as soon as the kingdoms of self and Satan have been thrown out. When the Lord moves in, it is more difficult for these enemy kingdoms to re-establish their reign.

We insist that the second priority in prayer that the Lord taught and wants is that His Kingdom should come. We declare that for that Kingdom to come the illegal kingdoms of self and Satan that occupy the place of the Kingdom of the Lord must be removed. These are taken out by prayer and deliberate action. When these have been taken out of the way, the Lord Jesus must be invited to move in and reign. He will move in and reign and wherever He reigns, the Kingdom of God has come!

Again as we said in the beginning, first, it is "Hallowed be Thy name." then it is "Thy kingdom come." Next it is going to be "Thy will be done." This gives God the first place in prayer, and when the first place is given to Him in anything, all else is blessed as far as that thing is concerned. Because true prayer begins with the giving of the triple first place to the Father, true prayer is the most blessed thing that can be done on this side of heaven.

Let us do it.

Let us do it God's way.

Let us begin now! Amen.

21

JESUS TAUGHT THEM THAT THE THIRD PRIORITY IN PRAYER IS TO PRAY THAT GOD'S WILL BE DONE ON EARTH AS IT IS IN HEAVEN

GOD'S WILL IS DONE IN HEAVEN

God's will was always done in heaven at the beginning. This went on for a long time. Then Satan rebelled and from that moment God's will was no longer being done in everything, by everyone in heaven. That state did not go on endlessly. There came a time when Satan and all the angels who had fallen with him, were thrown out of heaven. From the moment they were thrown out, things returned to normal. God's will was again done in perfection, by everyone in heaven. That has continued until today. At the very moment of writing, the will of God is being perfectly done in everything, by everyone, all the time in heaven. God's heart is fully satisfied with what is going on.

GOD'S WILL WAS DONE ON EARTH BY CHRIST

When Satan and his hosts were thrown out of heaven, they made the world their dwelling place. Their objective is to capture the hearts of people and lead them to oppose the will of God by doing their will.

The Lord Jesus came into the world as a challenge to Satan. He sought, knew and obeyed the Father's will in everything. He confessed again and again that He was totally free from any independence in action. He confessed that He only did the Father's will. He declared that he always put aside His own will in everything and did the Father's will. He confessed that He could not act until He had received instructions from His Father. He was utterly submissive.

The will of Jesus was not sinful. It was not twisted, yet in everything He put away His "correct and perfect will" and did that of the Father. The Lord Jesus was not seeking to do that which was correct. He was seeking to do that which was the Father's will. He, therefore, did not operate on the plane of rejecting that which was evil and doing that which was good. He operated on the plane of rejecting all that was the will of the devil, all that was the will of man, all that was His will; all that was good, better, best and all that was excellent. Only one thing mattered and only one thing was done and that one thing was the will of His Father.

THE RESOLUTE COMMITMENT TO DOING THE WILL OF THE FATHER, WHATEVER THAT WILL MAY BE, AND THE RESOLUTE REJECTION OF THE WILL OF THE DEVIL AND MAN, REGARDLESS OF WHAT THOSE WILLS MAY BE, CONSTITUTE A FORCE THAT BRINGS SATAN'S KINGDOM TO RUIN AND ESTABLISHES GOD'S KINGDOM IN MOST FAR-REACHING WAYS. THAT IS THE LIFE THAT JESUS LIVED, AND THAT IS THE LIFE TO WHICH WE HAVE BEEN CALLED.

GOD DESIRES HIS WILL DONE ON EARTH NOW

The Lord Jesus did God's will on earth in everything and the Father was satisfied. Today the Father again wants people who will do His will in everything.

The desire of His heart is that the adopted sons will be like the begotten Son in seeking, knowing and doing His will on earth. By this seeking, knowing and doing of His will, they would put His enemy totally to shame and to naught. That is the desire of the Father today. The question is whether He will find that type of obedience among the redeemed today.

If that type of obedience is going to be found among His today, it will not be found in the circles of those who have made it their primary duty to try and do God's will. Such will certainly fail. It will be found amongst those who, knowing that they are not able on their own, give themselves to prayer. Such will pray that the will of the Father be done on earth as it is in heaven. Such will pray that the will of the Father be done in their lives as it is done in heaven. As they pray, they will receive an inner love of the Father's will planted in their hearts by the Holy Spirit. That love will continue to be nourished as they continue in prayer until at some point, it possesses them. When the love of the Father's will will have possessed them, they will just put aside their own wills and give themselves to His will. They will find no sympathy in their hearts for the Enemy's will and so will reject it wholeheartedly. They will do God's will and they will do it increasingly. Then the Father will find people on earth who do His will as it is done in heaven.

This company of people who render to God total obedience in all things may begin with one person. However, as he prays and obeys, the Lord will add to him another person and another person and yet another person of the same obedient kind. As their number increases and as their prayer intensifies and their obedience becomes more complete, an army of obedient people will be raised to possess the earth for our God. This is victory.

Let us take, for example, that there are ten people on earth now who render total obedience to the Lord in everything and that it would take one year of prayer (each praying two hours a day) to produce another ten people in whose life the will of God would be done in a total way. Then we could have something like the following:

1990	10 people
1991	20
1992	40
1993	80
1994	160
1995	320
1996	640
1997	1,280
1998	2,560
1999	5,120
2000	10,240
2001	20,480
2002	40,960
2003	81,920
2004	163,840
2005	337,680
2006	675,360
2007	1,350,720
2008	2,701,440
2009	5,402,880

It is evident that, from ten people in 1989, the number of people who render total obedience to the Lord in all things and thus do the Father's will, could rise to over 5 million in twenty years. Could there be a more strategic plan for conquering the world for the Lord?

Could it be that the Lord is waiting for some ten people to start the wonderful world conquest through prayer crusades? Maybe you feel rather alone and you do not know others who are prepared to stand and to start with you. You do not have to give up. You need only to be sure that, as far as you know, you are doing God's will in all that He has shown you. You could then launch a personal crusade and let it go as follows:

1989	1
1990	2
1991	4
1992	8
1993	16
1994	32
1995	64
1996	128
1997	256
1998	512
1999	1,024
2000	2,048
2001	4,096
2002	8,192
2003	16,384
2004	32,768
2005	65,536
2006	131,072
2007	262,144
2008	524,288
2009	1,048,576
2010	2,097,152
2011	4,194,304
2012	8,388,604
2014	33,554,432
2015	67,108,864

It would mean that if the Lord tarries until 2015, that person would have brought over 67 million people to do the will of God on earth as it is in heaven.

I do not know that there can be a greater way of bringing the Lord's world to His feet. I find this possibility of World Conquest through Prayer (WCTP) the only real hope of ensuring that God's third priority is accomplished in prayer. I also see that if it is accomplished, it will positively affect the other two.

May the Lord help me to do something about it by beginning to pray for myself and for one person, along the lines we have mentioned in this chapter. May He help you to begin to pray for yourself and for one other person in the same way. May He move from heaven in might, multiply our efforts and then there will be a spiritual explosion; for there will then be multitudes of people in whose lives the will of God is done on earth as it is in heaven. Glory be to His name. Amen.

22

JESUS TAUGHT THEM TO PRAY FOR THEIR PERSONAL NEEDS THE PLACE OF PERSONAL NEEDS IN THE PRAYER LIFE

"*Give us each day our daily bread*" (Luke 11:3).

We have shown that God created prayer basically for the purpose of having His needs met. We have also shown that God created man so that he would find fullest fulfilment in knowing and serving God. That means that God created man in such a way that, for him to reach fullest potential, he had to forget himself entirely. The Lord even taught about this when He said, "*Therefore I tell you, do not be anxious about your life, what you shall eat or what you shall drink, nor about your body, what you shall put on. Is not life more than food, and the body more than clothing? Look at the birds of the air, they neither sow nor reap nor gather into barns, and yet your heavenly Father feeds them. Are you not of more value than they? And which of you by being anxious can add one cubit to his life span? And why are you anxious about clothing? Consider the lilies of the field, how they grow; they neither toil nor spin; yet I tell you, even Solomon in all his glory was not arrayed like one of these. But if God so clothes the grass of the field, which today is alive and tomorrow is thrown into the oven, will he not much more clothe you, O men of little faith? Therefore do not be anxious, saying, 'What shall we eat?' or 'What shall we drink?' or 'What shall we wear?' For the Gentiles need them all. But seek first his kingdom and his righteousness and all these things shall be yours as well. Therefore do not be anxious about tomorrow, for tomorrow will be anxious for itself. Let the day's own trouble be sufficient for the day*" (Matthew

6:25-34).

We have seen that the Lord has ordered that the priorities be: Hallowed be Thy name; Thy kingdom come; Thy will be done. If that is the case, and it is, we are likely to have four types of people.

The first class of people are those who become so preoccupied with the hallowing of God's name, the coming of God's Kingdom and the doing of God's will that they do not have time to ask anything else of God. It is not that they do not want to ask the Lord for their daily bread. It is just that when they have a two, three or four hour session and enter into God's presence in prayer, their eyes are so opened to the needs of God's holiness, kingdom and will that they give themselves to these. They will not have finished praying about these when the time in prayer is totally exhausted and they must move on to the next thing. While they are moving to the next thing, they are still burdened and still "occupied" with continued and unceasing prayer to God for His holiness, Kingdom and will, that there is no time for anything else. Soon what they are doing is over and they are back into God's presence to labour in prayer for His name, Kingdom and will. It becomes obvious that such, because they are so carried away with God and have no time left to plead their case and pray for their needs in detail, will have God move on their behalf. A simple prayer from such that says, "Lord, give me each day of this week, month, year, my daily bread," will be sufficient, and the God who feeds the ravens that do His will but do not pray for their daily bread, will become carried away with their needs. He knows their needs and will supply each one of them. NO ONE CAN BECOME PREOCCUPIED WITH PRAYING FOR GOD'S NEEDS AND GOD DOES NOT BECOME PREOCCUPIED WITH THE PERSON'S NEEDS.

There are very few who attain unto such a high level of being preoccupied with God. Consequently, there are few who give God the opportunity to become totally preoccupied with their personal needs.

The second class are believers who divide their time carefully. They spend some of it praying for the needs of God His holiness, Kingdom and will and then they turn and pray systematically for their own needs. I think that most maturing believers are here.

The third class are believers who see too little of God's needs, and so they may pray a little about God's holiness, Kingdom and will, but they soon turn to their needs and pray for them in detail. If they spend one hour in prayer, they may pray for the Lord's needs in five minutes and for their own needs in fifty-five minutes. They pray about God's needs in a general and vague way and pray for their needs with clarity and in specific detail. They expect God to answer the prayers they are making to Him about His name, Kingdom and will. They are able to exercise faith about their own needs being met, but they are not able to exercise any faith about the needs of God; for no one can exercise faith about issues that are vague in his mind. I say with pain in my heart that most believers who pray are in this class.

The fourth class of believers pray vaguely about their needs. They do not pray about God's needs because they do not even know that God has needs. They cannot concentrate in prayer. They jump from one issue to the other. They pray, "My Lord, bless me, bless my wife, our children and our car. Bless my job and help me to get promoted and have a rise in salary. God, bless our neighbours. Protect us from danger and sudden death. Bless the food we eat and keep us from all deadly diseases. Thank you, Lord, in Jesus' name."

It is sad to say that there are many true believers who, even after many years in the Lord, pray like this. This is a shame. The last class only utters a few words to God at moments of crisis.

PERSONAL NEEDS AS GOD'S NEEDS

There is a point in spiritual growth and spiritual union with God that the needs of God and the needs of man become indivisible. When a person attains that level of growth and union, he will find that he cannot pray for God's holiness without being concerned about his own holiness; that he cannot pray about the Kingdom of God coming without praying that his own kingdom be caused to disappear; and that he cannot pray about God's will being done without praying that his own will should be put aside completely.

Seen from this perspective, it becomes as important for the believer to pray for his own needs as it is for him to pray for God's needs; and failure to pray for his own needs will result in failure to pray for God's needs in totality.

Take, for example, the praying for daily bread. The consecrated believer will eat so as to do the will of God in good health. His health then becomes important for the doing of God's will. He will pray for his food which will influence his health, not merely because he wants a strong and healthy body, but because that body is important for the accomplishment of God's will. In that sense, someone who invests his life praying for the feeding and providing of food for a servant of the Lord is doing holy work; for were such a one to feed badly, he could become sick and disabled or even die and, as a result, bring great loss to the service of the Lord.

When things are seen that way, then there can be no division between the spiritual and the physical; between food for the spirit and food for the soul and body; between praying for a man's spiritual walk and his bodily health, all is held in harmony, and all is held in prayer.

This means that there may be some who are called by the Lord not to "serve tables" but to "give themselves to prayer and the ministry of the word." Such may be totally carried away with praying for God's holiness, Kingdom and will, while others are raised by the Lord to pray for and supply the daily bread of these and, therefore, the needs of the whole body are met.

For this to be so, prayer and all other areas of Christian service must be seen not just as the work of individuals, but as the work of the Church. This means that no one will try to do everything, but each one will seek the Lord, receive from Him his place in the Body and serve at that place. In that way the needs of everyone will be met. Glory be to the Lord! Amen.

23

JESUS TAUGHT THEM TO PRAY FOR THEIR PERSONAL NEEDS ASKING FOR DAILY BREAD AND OTHER DAILY NEEDS

"*Give us each day our daily bread*" (Luke 11:3).

The disciples were encouraged by the Lord to ask for their daily material needs. He used bread as representative of all that they would need in the practical living of each day.

What should the disciple ask about daily bread?

The disciple should ask for his needs and not for his wants. God has committed Himself to provide the needs and not the wants of the disciple. He has committed Himself to provide the wants and not the luxuries of the believer. "*YOUR HEAVENLY FATHER KNOWS THAT YOU NEED THEM ALL*" (Matthew 6:32). The heavenly Father knows that you need food, clothing and drink and He counsels that His children should not be anxious about these. He says, "*Therefore do not be anxious, saying, 'What shall we eat?' or 'What shall we drink?' or 'What shall we wear?'* " (Matthew 6:31). The Apostle Paul wrote, "*There is great gain in godliness with contentment; for we brought nothing into the world, and we cannot take anything out of the world; but if we have food and clothing, with these we shall be content. But those who desire to be rich fall into temptation, into a snare, into many senseless and hurtful desires that plunge men into ruin and destruction. For the love of money is the root of all evils; it is through this craving that some have wandered away from the faith and pierced their hearts with many pangs*" (1 Timothy 6:6-10).

So the believer must settle in his heart that he is to ask for his needs and not his wants. He has no mandate from the Lord to ask for things that will satisfy the covetousness of his heart. Food and clothing are seen by the Lord as the believer's needs. The Apostle Paul also confirms that these are the needs of a believer and that with these the believer is to be content.

Looking at it in other terms, the believer is to pray for the holiness of God's name, the Kingdom of God and his personal material needs of food and clothing. Those who are caught up with God's holiness, Kingdom and will have no time to ask for the things that will advance indulgence of the heart.

We can see that each generation is becoming more indulgent than the previous one. This is manifested in the fact that each generation is less satisfied than the previous one. The preceding generation might have wanted food in order to do the business of life. Their needs were, consequently, simple and easy to supply. The present generation is not eating to do the business of life. It has made eating the business of life. Because this is so, there is preoccupation with different types of foods; so that in some countries, a good bread shop will have forty to fifty different types of bread; so that people may have increased opportunity to manifest the corruption of their hearts. Clothes are no longer for covering and protecting the body. They are being made to satisfy the changing tastes of a generation that has divorced itself from God and is seeking happiness where it cannot be found. No one who has truly met the Lord who gave His all to make poor people become rich, can join the world in this madness. The committed believer will ensure that he is not trapped in the desire for more and more, regardless of his environment. He will choose the simple life. He will cut down his clothing to a minimum. He will cut down his food to what is needed to keep him alive and strong in the service of the Lord. He will refuse to be caught up with the mad striving for variety that is all around. He will be a man apart, totally apart.

He will be so related to the Lord that he will find his joy increasingly in Him and less and less in what the world has to offer.

This has an effect on prayer. I believe that the prayers of a very contented man have greater impact than those of a less contented man. The contented man looks wholeheartedly to the Lord and the things being asked for in prayer, whereas the discontented man is divided at heart. He does not know whether He wants Jesus or he wants things.

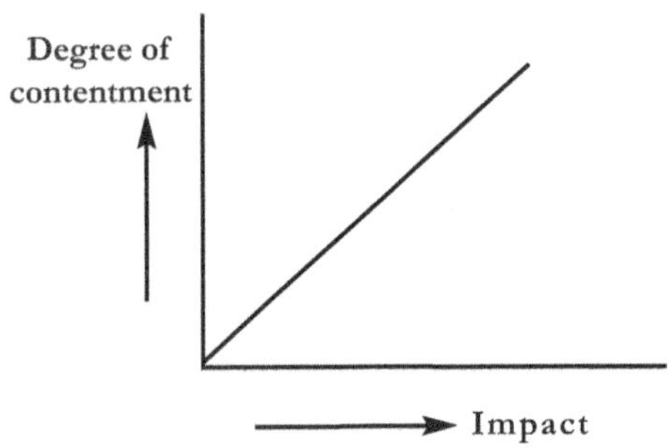

The Relationship between the Degree of Contentment and the Impact of the Person's Prayer

There are variations in how much a person needs to be contented and the impact of his prayer life. The person who is contented with very little is more powerful in prayer than the person who needs more to be contented. We can illustrate this as follows:

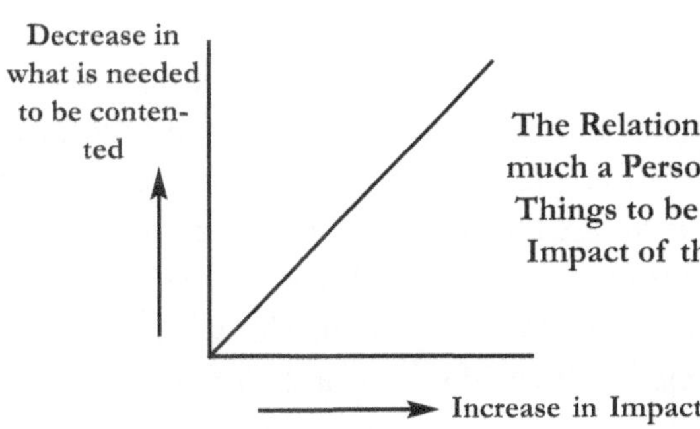

The Relationship between How much a Person Needs of Wordly Things to be contented and the Impact of the Person's Prayer

We can say that impact is inversely proportional to what a person needs in order to be contented. The person who needs more in order to be contented will pray, but his prayers will produce less impact than the person who needs less. So the more things you accumulate, the more things that are given to you which you keep for yourself, the longer your market list, the more the variety of things on your dining table, the less impact is being produced by your prayers.

One just needs to look at the lives of those whose prayers made impact for God, and it will soon be realized that they were people who possessed little of the world's goods. Some of them could have possessed many things but they decided to give them away to others. The supreme example of this is the Lord Jesus. He was enormously rich but gave away all His wealth for our sake and became poor that we might be rich. The far-reaching consequences of His prayers need no further mention. Another example is the Apostle Paul. He could have been very rich but, because of Christ, he counted everything as loss and became poor that he might serve the Lord and the Church, thereby, making many rich. We know the far-reaching consequences of his prayers. Then we can think of Anna who lived in the temple for sixty or more years. She could not have possessed much. What of Elijah? He did not have much. The Lord had to send a raven to feed him and later on, the widow had to receive a miracle so that she could meet both her needs and his. In Church history, people like John Knox, Praying Hyde, Braneird, Pastor His, John Sung, Howard Rees, Watchman Nee, Hudson Taylor, to name only a few of God's praying generals, were all men who deliberately gave themselves to a life of utter simplicity.

I am of the opinion that things occupy the heart and block both the channels for revelation and prayer. A man is not quite the same after he has acquired an additional thing. Each thing leads to the desire for the next. Take, for example, the purchase of a car. It brings with it the needs to purchase a road license, an insurance policy, a garage and perhaps some special device to keep away thieves. Each of these things is an extra weight that could cloud the mind and limit communion with God.

There is so much covetousness in our day under the cover of things that are needed for the spread of the Gospel. We can imitate and compete with each other and amass enormous quantities of things. Some a few of them are needs. The rest are hindrances. Our technological age with so much advance in the application of modern technology to the Gospel ministry, has in no way helped to outclass the disciples of the Lord in the first century in the relative quality and quantity of the results obtained. We must face the fact that our real need is not more things and newer methods. Our real need is the presence and power of God. This presence and power is not advanced by the presence of material things. If anything, an excess of things will stand in the way.

This means that although we have been invited to make request for our needs, the disciplined cut down their possessions to the barest minimum and, as they spend more time with God, they are able to concentrate on the priorities, which are God's holiness, Kingdom and will.

What then should a person who loves the Lord do? We answer that he should reduce his needs to a minimum and should labour to ensure that he does not increase them. He should labour to be content with a little. He should not accept things and use them simply because they are given to him. He should give away much of what he is receiving. He should ask for food, clothing and transportation. He should ask for money for postage, literature, furniture, and the rest of the things that he needs. He should ask himself before he acquires anything: "Will I be the same after I have acquired this thing or will the possession of it place a weight on my spirit? Is there someone I know who needs it more than I do? If the trumpet were to blow today and I were to stand before the Judgment Seat of Christ to give account of my possessions, would I gladly give account of possessing this particular thing? Would Jesus have acquired this same thing were He living in my day?" Such questions will help clarify the motives of the heart and help the honest person to live rightly. May the Lord help us to so ask.

If we are consecrated and truly disciplined, seeking heavenly things and using only those earthly things that are truly necessary to enable us to accomplish the call of God on our lives, we shall soon see that we do not have many things to ask the Lord for in the realm of daily bread and daily needs. We shall find that we have time to concentrate on praying that His name be hallowed, His Kingdom come, and His will be done. Then we shall be truly blessed. Praise the Lord!

I DO NOT QUITE KNOW WHAT I NEED

After many years of asking God for my daily needs I was surprised to realize that I had been making a dangerous assumption for more than twenty years. In coming to the Lord with a list of what I thought were my needs I was assuming that I knew what my needs were. I have to acknowledge with shame that I do not know what my needs are. The Lord knows what my needs are more than I do. He knows more than I know and sees what I do not see. His knowledge of my needs is, consequently, greater and better than mine.

This knowledge has been quite revolutionary for me. I no longer sit down and think out what I suppose my needs for the day and the days ahead will be. I instead go before Him with pen and paper and ask Him to show me what my needs are and what they will be. As He shows me my needs I write them down and then I pray to Him, pleading that He should supply them. This has brought revolutionary results. I have been led to know needs that I could not have known on my own and been led not to ask for things that I thought were needs but which later on were seen not to be needs.

Take, for example, that a brother writes that his wife, his six children and he are coming to spend two weeks with my family. If I am using my head, I will work out the needed additional space, food, and other things as my needs and ask the Lord in prayer to supply them. I may begin to make various arrangements following the reasoning of my mind. On the day before the promised day, I could receive a letter from the brother saying that because of new opportunities to reach out for Christ, the promised journey is cancelled. I then do not need the things I was asking in preparation for them. If, on the other hand, upon receipt of his letter I had gone to the Lord, spread it before Him and read it to Him and then asked him to show me what my needs were, He would have revealed that I needed just what is enough for my own family. I would have written what He showed me were my needs and then I would have prayed them through. I would have had to believe Him that what was enough for one family would be made sufficient for the two families. When the letter cancelling the trip came, I would have known why He did not show me that I needed the extra things. I would have been spared the burden of unnecessary prayers and preparation, and concentrated on His name, Kingdom and will as usual.

This to me is revolutionary. However, it calls for the discipline of waiting before God, hearing His voice, discerning His voice, believing that one has actually heard Him, walking by faith and trusting the Lord. It also calls for an end to man's greed; for the Lord will not reveal to anyone that the person needs what he does not need.

Are you prepared for this revolutionary walk with God?

I am writing this message on July 7th, 1989. On the 25th of July, I will go on a missionary trip of forty days that will enable me to minister to the Lord and the Lord's people in Uganda, Kenya, India, Israel, France and Spain. How can I, by using my imagination, know what my needs will be in these countries? I have not been to four of these countries before and even where I have visited before, I cannot predict what things will be like this time. I have only one clear path opened to me. I must ask the Lord to show me what will be my needs for each day of the trip. I will also ask Him to show me what my needs will be in each country I will visit. I will ask Him what my needs will be for each meeting I will hold and, by His grace, I will write out my prayer topics and then pray. I have already begun to ask Him, receive from Him and pray. I will do so until it is departure time and then I will go and continue to do so until I have completed the journey and accomplished what He is sending me out to do for Him. And then I will come back and spend many days in thanksgiving. Glory be to His holy name. Amen.

24

JESUS TAUGHT THEM TO PRAY FOR THEIR PERSONAL NEEDS ASKING FOR FORGIVENESS

"*And forgive us our sins*" (Luke 11:4).

One thing that surprised me at the beginning of this study was that the Lord did not teach the disciples to start with "And forgive us our sins." The truth is that that is what I have done for the last twenty-two years. I began my prayer sessions with trying to find out if there were any unconfessed sins in my life and if I found any, I would confess them before I felt worthy to talk to God about anything else. However, we see the Lord placing things in a different order. He puts God's holiness, Kingdom and will first, and then comes to man's needs of food and other practical needs, before He comes to man's need of forgiveness.

What is the meaning of this? Is the Lord teaching that if a person commits sin and it is weighing on him, he should pretend that it is not there and first pray about God's holiness, Kingdom and will, followed by his practical needs before he comes to ask and receive forgiveness from God? By no means. The Lord understands that in the life of a normal believer, when sin is committed, the believer will feel so bad and be so broken that he should seek the Lord at once, repent of his sin before Him, confess it to Him and receive forgiveness and restoration into fellowship. Such a one will then have had his sin thoroughly dealt with before his normal prayer time comes. He will then come to God with no sin against him that he knows of. He will come with a clear conscience, plug into God and begin to enjoy fellowship with Him, praying for His holiness, Kingdom and will, and presenting his personal needs in prayer to the Lord. In the course of his fellowship with God the light of God will dawn upon his soul in greater clarity. He will then see himself and the things that he did before coming into the presence of the Lord differently. He will find that, having now received more light, there were things that he did wrong that he did not know were wrong. He will also now see that there were things that he ought to have done which he did not do the sins of omission, for which he should seek forgiveness from the Lord.

So the man came before the Lord with a clear conscience. Before the Lord, things have been revealed and the conscience is no longer clear. Forgiveness must be sought and received.

The Apostle John put all this together in a beautiful way when he wrote, "*This is the message we heard from him and proclaim to you, that God is light and in him is no darkness at all. If we say we have fellowship with him while we walk in darkness, we lie and do not live according to the truth; but if we walk in the light, as he is in the light, we have fellowship with one another, and the blood of Jesus his Son cleanses us from all sin. If we say we have no sin, we deceive ourselves and the truth is not in us. If we confess our sins, he is faithful and just, and will forgive our sins and cleanse us from all unrighteousness*" (1 John 1:5-9).

It is those who, from the beginning, are walking in the light who now see the need for the cleansing of the blood, because the light has exposed some darkness. If after some darkness has been exposed a person does not want to repent and seek cleansing and forgiveness, he gets out of touch with God and further praying becomes self-deception.

In asking for forgiveness a person must be very specific. It is useless to ask the Lord to forgive you for failing Him without telling Him how, when and where you failed Him. Those who confess sin in a general way will receive general forgiveness which is actually no forgiveness. Whereas, those who confess sin in a specific way will receive specific forgiveness, which is true forgiveness.

Many believers are so dishonest with man that they think that they can carry out the same dishonesty with God. They have never learnt to be transparent. They have never learnt to call things by name. Suppose your son came to you weeping and said, "My father, forgive me for this evil that I have done. Just be merciful and forgive me. I am wrong. I am all wrong. My heart is distorted. Please forgive me. I will not do it again. I will never do it again." How will you feel? Will you forgive him? Of what does he want to be forgiven? Unless he gets down to details: "I did this and this and that; I did it here and there; I did it to this extent; I did it at such a time; I did it for this reason and I did it in the companionship of such a person, and so on," it would be meaningless to forgive him.

Those who do not confess sin in detail to the Lord and if need be, to man; find it relatively easier to fall back into the same sin, whereas detail and frank confession puts the Enemy to shame and to flight.

The Lord invites the believer to come to Him and be forgiven. There is no reason to get into the presence of the Lord with a good conscience, see your life in the light of His light and go away from the Lord with a bad conscience because the sin revealed by His presence has not been confessed and forgiveness received. In fact, a person ought to come out of the Lord's presence in better spiritual health than when he went in.

I have found that after I have confessed my sins to the Lord and asked Him to forgive me, I wait before Him. After that I ask Him if I have been forgiven. He does give me the assurance that I am forgiven. If He thus assures me, I turn back to Him and ask Him to restore me to deep and vital fellowship with Him. I wait before Him in silence and then I receive assurance that I am restored.

There are times when I do ask Him if I am forgiven and His answer is, "No." I then ask Him where I am not forgiven. Sometimes He has told me that I have only thrown my sin before Him without real repentance. At such times I have begged Him to give me the gift of true repentance. In His love He has always given me when I asked. I was then able to repent as I should and when that happened, His forgiveness was immediate and my joy was full. At other times, He has shown me that He could not forgive me because I had confessed some sin or sins and left out one or more unconfessed. When I knew what I did not confess, I confessed it. However, there have been times when I did not know what I had left unconfessed. I then asked Him to show me and He did. I was then able to confess what was not confessed and then receive forgiveness for all. Sometimes He has shown that I confessed the act of sin but did not repent of my attitude towards the sin. I was then able to repent both of the act and then of my attitude towards the sin and then to receive His gracious forgiveness and restoration.

How good our God is! How wonderful His tender love and mercy are towards us! He deserves limitless praise. Amen.

25

JESUS TAUGHT THEM TO PRAY FOR THEIR PERSONAL NEEDS FORGIVENESS GRANTED

"*For we ourselves forgive everyone who is indebted to us*" (Luke 11:4).

The Lord links our receiving forgiveness from Him to the fact that we have forgiven others. The Word of God is very plain about this and the importance of the matter is shown in the fact that it is taught in many places in the Word.

1. Mark 11:25: "*And when you stand praying, forgive, if you have anything against anyone; so that your Father also who is in heaven may forgive your trespasses.*"
2. Matthew 6:14-15: "*And if you forgive men their trespasses, your heavenly Father also will forgive you; but if you do not forgive men their trespasses, neither will your Father forgive your trespasses.*"
3. Matthew 18:23-35: "*Therefore the kingdom of heaven may be compared to a king who wishes to settle accounts with his servants. When he began the reckoning, one was brought to him who owed him ten thousand talents; and as he could not pay, his lord ordered him to be sold, with his wife and children and all that he had, and payment to be made. So the servant fell on his knees, imploring him, 'Lord, have patience with me, and I will pay you everything.' And out of pity for him the lord of that servant released him and forgave him the debt. But that same servant, as he went out, came upon one of his fellow servants who owed him a hundred denarii; and seizing him by the throat he said, 'Pay what you owe.' So his fellow servant fell down and besought him, 'Have patience with me, and I will pay you.' He*

refused and went and put him in prison till he should pay the debt. When his fellow servants saw what had taken place, they were greatly distressed, and they went and reported to their lord all that had taken place. Then his lord summoned him and said to him, 'You wicked servant! I forgave you all that debt because you besought me; and should not you have had mercy on your fellow servant, as I had mercy on you?' And in anger his lord delivered him to the jailers, till he should pay all his debt. So also my heavenly Father will do to every one of you, if you do not forgive your brother from your heart."

The Lord Jesus taught in all the three passages above. His message is clear. ANYONE WHO WILL NOT FORGIVE ANOTHER PERSON WHO HAS WRONGED HIM WILL NOT BE FORGIVEN BY THE HEAVENLY FATHER. ANYONE WHO IS NOT FORGIVEN BY THE HEAVENLY FATHER IS ABIDING IN DEATH. ANYONE ABIDING IN DEATH PRAYS IN VAIN. HE CANNOT BE HEARD, FOR GOD DOES NOT LISTEN TO THE NOISE OF A SPIRITUAL CORPSE.

NO CHOICE ABOUT FORGIVING

A person does not forgive the person who has wronged him in order to do that one a favour. He forgives the person because he himself needs the blessings that flow from forgiving the person. In Mark's Gospel, the Lord says that a person should forgive so that he himself may be forgiven. The person who does not forgive is automatically not forgiven. In Matthew's Gospel the Lord teaches clearly that the one who does not forgive will not be forgiven. In the same parable, the Lord Jesus shows that the person who does not forgive will have all the past sins which he has committed and been forgiven of, imputed to him. That is, if a person had sinned one million times and been forgiven totally but refuses to forgive another person, he will not only not be forgiven in the future, but all the one million sins that had been forgiven will be imputed to him permanently. This means that for a believer not to forgive is for him to demand that all his sins be put on him; so that his condition before God is like that of one who has never believed! This is most serious. It shows that those who do not forgive have received only a temporal forgiveness. It can be taken away from them. For anyone to toy with not forgiving another is to play with death.

FORGIVENESS FROM THE HEART

The Lord does not demand forgiveness from the lips only, but He wants forgiveness from the heart. This means that the forgiveness must be complete and it must be thorough. It must not be conditional.

This type of forgiveness implies that the forgiven person is treated from the heart as if he had never sinned. He is not just treated outwardly as if he had never sinned. He is not just treated outwardly as if he is forgiven. He is forgiven inwardly in a complete way and treated outwardly as the totally forgiven one that he is.

Below are the marks of the forgiveness from the heart:

1. It is total.
2. It is complete.
3. It is without reserve.
4. It is unconditional.
5. The forgiven party is restored to all the rights that he had before he sinned.
6. The forgiven party is blessed.
7. Nothing of the sin that was committed by the forgiven party is ever mentioned to man or to God.

Anyone who has not or does not forgive in this way has not forgiven at all. His own sins will not be forgiven and all past sins are upon him.

FORGIVING OTHERS AND THE PRAYER LIFE

The impact of a person's prayer is not proportional to the extent to which he has forgiven others. The person who knowingly refuses to forgive even one person is totally blocked. His prayers are a sheer waste of time.

FORGIVING THE UNREPENTANT

The question may arise as to whether forgiveness is to be dished out to unrepentant people. The answer is, "Yes." The Lord Jesus Christ on the cross forgave those who crucified Him and pleaded that the Father should forgive them. They had not repented and yet He pleaded that they be forgiven. That is the example for us to follow.

When we forgive a person, we unbind him from his bonds. This gives him freedom to come to himself and to see the gravity of his sin and thus to repent.

When a person does not forgive another, he binds the person and binds himself and labours, thereby, to bring two lives to naught. God forbid.

A PERSONAL QUESTION

Do you know of anyone on planet Earth whom you hold something against in your heart? If there is such a person, forgive him at once before you do another thing. Forgive him before you utter the next word of prayer to God. If not, you labour absolutely in vain.

If you forgive the person from the heart, let him know. Confess to God that you have forgiven the person. Confess also to the person that he is forgiven and, how blessed you will be!

26

JESUS TAUGHT THEM TO PRAY FOR THEIR PERSONAL NEEDS LEAD US NOT INTO TEMPTATION!

"*And lead us not into temptation*" (Luke 11:4).

The Bible says of the Lord Jesus that He was led by the Spirit into the wilderness to be tempted by the devil (Luke 4:1). It says of the Lord that "*For because he himself has suffered and been tempted, he is able to help those who are tempted*" (Hebrews 2:18). "*For we have not a high priest who is unable to sympathize with our weaknesses, but one who in every respect has been tempted as we are, yet without sin*" (Hebrews 4:15).

There are two parts to a temptation. The first part is that of testing. In that part the person being tempted is being given the opportunity to choose between God's way and the devil's way. The purpose of this aspect of temptation is that the person may, by the choice he makes, prove or manifest what his character is. The first part of temptation is best called trial. It is this that Peter writes about when he says: "*In this you rejoice, though now for a little while you may have to suffer various trials, so that the genuineness of your faith, more precious than gold which though perishable is tested by fire, may rebound to praise and glory and honour at the revelation of Jesus Christ*" (1 Peter 1:6-7). It is about this that James wrote, saying: "*Count it all joy, my brethren, when you meet various trials, for you know that the testing of your faith produces steadfastness. And let steadfastness have its full effect, that you may be perfect and complete, lacking nothing*" (James 1:2-4).

We can illustrate what we are saying as follows :

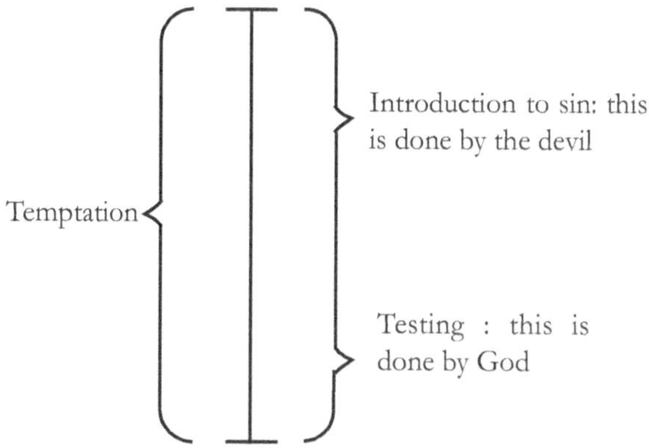

What the two Aspects of Temptation are

WHAT THE TWO ASPECTS OF TEMPTATION ARE

In testing, the possibilities are presented to a person so that he may choose according to the intentions of his heart. This is what God did with Abraham. The Bible says, "*After these things God tested Abraham and said to him, 'Abraham!' And he said, 'Here I am.' He said, 'Take your son, your only son Isaac whom you love, and go to the land of Moriah, and offer him there as a burnt offering upon one of the mountains of which I shall tell you'* " (Genesis 22:1-2). God was testing Abraham. He simply asked him to carry out costly obedience, and left it to Abraham to choose whether or not to obey. The Lord did not pressurize Abraham in any way. He was left alone as a free moral agent to make his choice. He chose to obey the Lord and overcame the temptation by passing the test.

God, who cannot sin, does test people, but He cannot induce them to sin. The devil may begin to test a person, but if he finds that the person is passing the test, he will not leave it there. He will move unto the second stage and begin to seduce the person to sin.

God uses His testing and the devil's inductions or seductions to sin to classify people.

EVERY COMMAND IS A TESTING

God's examination for spiritual progress goes on daily. Every command demands obedience which immediately leads to spiritual promotion. It also carries with it the possibility of disobedience, which will lead to spiritual demotion.

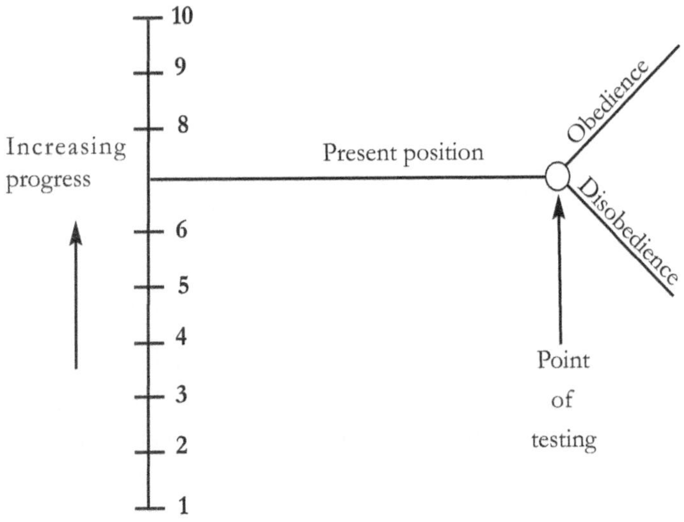

What Happens in Testing

No one who disobeys the Lord is the same after he has disobeyed. He is demoted because of his disobedience, while the obedient is promoted because of his obedience. This means that two people who are at the same spiritual level may soon be far apart after a series of tests. We can illustrate it as follows:

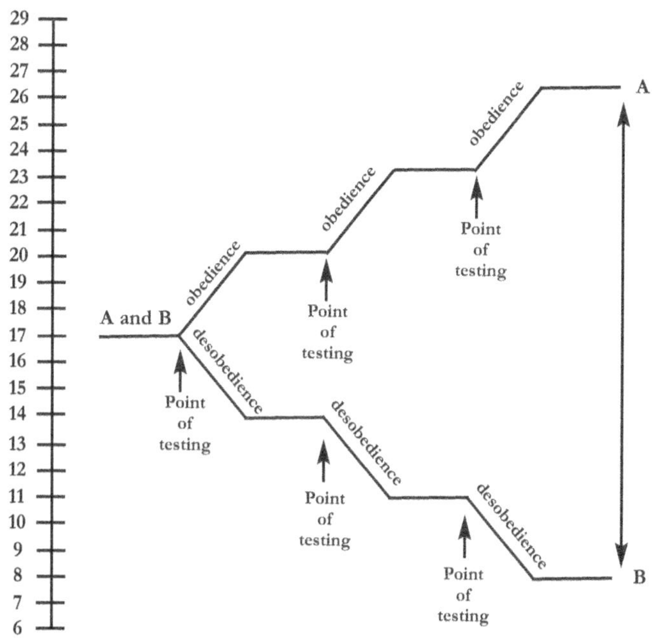

The Impact of Three Consecutive Acts of Obedience and Desobedience

Since testing is God's way of examining His children for progress, there is no way that anyone can run away from being tested. God's testings should be welcome.

THE DEVIL CAN CONVERT TESTING INTO INDUCTION TO SIN

God wants to evaluate. The evaluation will lead to promotion, depending on what is on a man's heart. Man is left free to choose. The devil also evaluates. From the beginning he may just test a person. If the person fails the test by yielding to sin, then his job is through. If, on the other hand, the person wins the test by not yielding to the sin, he is frustrated and furious. He now takes over and no longer leaves the person aside to choose for himself. He begins to pressurize the person, inducing and seducing him to sin. He will use every opportunity that he can use. It is no more a testing. It is pressure to sin. He wants only one result that the person should fall into temptation. The believer is, as it were, under the pressure of the evil one.

LEAD US NOT INTO TEMPTATION

It is at this point that the prayer of the believer that the Lord should not lead him into temptation makes sense. He is pleading, "Lord, do not allow me to be taken over by Satan in a situation in which You are testing me. I accept Your testing, but Lord, do not allow Satan to take over, so that all pressure is being brought upon me to sin. I may be able to win when You test me, but I am not sure that I will not fail when Satan takes over and begins to use every possible way to induce me to sin. Lord, do not leave me alone. Stand with me. Lord, stand with me; I need You. I need You so that Satan should not overcome me. Lord, lead me not into temptation. Lord, lead me not to the point where Satan takes over.

THE LORD DOES ANSWER SUCH PRAYERS

If the Lord asked the disciples to pray that He should not lead them into temptation, then He meant to say that He is prepared to answer such prayers. It means that the person who does not have confidence in himself but fears that he may fail under severe pressure from Satan, will ask the Lord to preserve him from such pressures. The Lord will answer and he will not be led into the pressures that are beyond him. He will, consequently, only be brought by the Lord into situations in which he will pass the test and be promoted by the Lord.

All this means that those who do not pray not to be led into temptation are confessing that they can overcome in any situation.

Such boasting is in the flesh. It is the lot of those who do not know themselves and who do not know the devil. They are too proud to pray, and soon they will find that they have yielded to sin and sunk to levels that they could not have imagined.

I rarely hear the people of God pray asking the Lord not to lead them into temptation. For a long time I myself never prayed that way. I have, however, learnt my lessons and repented. The great extent to which the people of God today commit sin can partly be attributed to the fact that they have not taken the Lord Jesus seriously and, therefore, not prayed accordingly. May those who have ears to hear, hear. May the teachers teach the younger ones to pray as the Lord, in sovereign wisdom, taught. Then the Lord will not lead His into temptation and the devil will not have an opportunity to pressurize them into sin.

Do something about it today. Before you go out in the morning, pray asking the Lord not to lead you into temptation. When facing every new situation in the day, pray again in the same manner. When you are going to meet someone you have not met before, pray that prayer, for he might be Satan's agent to tempt you to sin and pressurize you that way. When you are going to meet a friend, do not say, "I am going to meet my friend. He loves the Lord. Satan can have no part in our meeting." Such talk is foolish talk. The Enemy delights to take people unawares; for then he has greater chances of success. He is present in the holiest assembly. He is present at the most serious prayer meeting of the most consecrated believers. He appears even in the presence of God. He is prepared to appear as an angel of light, if that will help him. So, do not take chances. Pray before every situation that the Lord should not lead you into temptation. He will do it, and the triumph will be yours to enjoy. Praise the Lord! Amen.

27

JESUS TAUGHT THEM TO PRAY FOR THEIR PERSONAL NEEDS DELIVER US FROM THE EVIL ONE

"*But deliver us from the evil one*" (Matthew 6:13).

We have shown that the Lord does try or test a person to see if he is fit for promotion. Who would not test a structure before he puts weight on it? We also saw that the Lord tests without inducing the person to sin, that the person is left on his own as a moral agent to choose what he wants.

We also saw that the devil can test a person. If he finds the person to be coming through the test victoriously, he will put pressure on him and do all he can to induce the person to fail. Thus the devil always starts with testing but inevitably ends up pressurizing those who would not yield, to yield. The result is that those who are led into temptation find themselves in the hands of the evil one.

Satan even sometimes asks God to allow him to prove that some persons are not sincere in their relationship with God. He accused Job, "*Does Job fear God for nought? Has thou not put a hedge about him and his house and all that he has on every side? Thou hast blessed the work of his hands, and his possessions have increased in the land. But put forth thy hand now, and touch all that he has, and he will curse thee to thy face. 'And the Lord said to Satan, 'Behold, all that he has is in your power; only upon himself do not put forth your hand.' So Satan went forth from the presence of the Lord*" (Job 1:9-12).

Satan went away to make arrangements so that all that Job had was lost in one day! The arrangements worked, and in one day Job lost everything that he possessed. He also lost all his sons and daughters. He was in the hands of the evil one. Satan was the author of all that he was suffering but he acted under permission. The Lord drew the limits beyond which he could not tempt him. The limits were, "Upon himself do not put forth your hand." Satan could not defy those limits without permission. He came for the permission to do so.

The Bible says, "*Again there was a day when the sons of God came to present themselves before the Lord, and Satan also came among them to present himself before the Lord. And the Lord said to Satan, 'Whence have you come?' Satan answered the Lord, 'From going to and fro on the earth, and from walking up and down on it.' And the Lord said to Satan, 'Have you considered my servant Job, that there is none like him on earth, a blameless and upright man, who fears God and turns away from evil? He still holds fast his integrity, although you have moved me against him, to destroy him without cause.' Then Satan answered the Lord, 'Skin for skin! All that a man has he will give for his life. But put forth thy hand now, and touch his bone and his flesh, and he will curse thee to thy face.' And the Lord said to Satan, 'Behold, he is in your power; only spare his life'*" (Job 2:1-6). Satan went forth to afflict Job's body although he could not kill him because the Lord had drawn the limits and Satan has no power to bypass the limits that God has given him.

We now see that a believer can be in the hands of the evil one, even as Job was. That is the reason for which he needs to cry to the Lord, "Deliver me from the evil one."

DANGEROUS IGNORANCE

Job was a blameless and upright man who feared God and turned away from evil. He was a man who held his integrity under times of severe temptation. However, Job was not experienced in spiritual warfare. For example, it was the Lord who "*Put a hedge about him and his house and all that he has on every side*" (Job 1:10). He did nothing to reinforce the hedge. He did not co-operate with God so that as the Lord built the hedge he, too, would build it. It is as if the Lord built the hedge from inside and expected Job to build it from outside. If he had done this, probably the devil would not have "seen" him and all that he had to begin to make suggestions about them being reasons for his integrity.

Secondly, when he was attacked by Satan, he just submitted passively to it. He did not sin, which is good. However, he did not resist. The Bible commands us, saying, "*Resist the devil and he will flee from you*" (James 4:7). He did not only resist the devil, he also did not ask the Lord to deliver him from the evil one. He left everything in the hands of God. He was ignorant and, consequently, he was passive where he ought to have been active and even offensive. God will draw the limits to which the devil may go in harassing His children. However, those who are passive and submit to the devil, may suffer more than they should.

WHAT HAPPENS IN THE UNSEEN

It is important that the believer should understand something of what happens in the unseen. Let us take one example. The Bible says, "*Satan stood up against Israel, and incited David to number Israel*" (1 Chronicles 21:1). Satan wanted to destroy people in Israel. He asked the Lord for permission to be allowed to incite David to number the people and, thereby, be the reason for the subsequent judgment. The Lord allowed him.

In 2 Samuel 21:1, the Bible says, "Again the anger of the Lord was kindled against Israel, and he incited David against them, saying, 'Go, number Israel and Judah.'" David did and there were disastrous results.

What happened is that Satan asked God for permission to incite

David; for God can never incite anyone to take a decision that would be destructive. However, although the Lord allowed Satan it appeared as if He himself did it. In the matter of Job, the Lord said, "*You have moved me against him*" (Job 2:3). So the Lord considers that He is the one acting when He permits the devil to do something. That is why He allowed it to be recorded in 2 Samuel that it was God's anger that was kindled against Israel and He incited David to number them to their undoing.

Because of what is happening in the unseen, believers must be informed and they must refuse to be passive. The devil wants to do harm. He has many plans for evil. If he is allowed, he will do harm. There are a number of things that the believer must do. The following are some:

1. He should build a hedge in prayer around himself, his household and all that he has on every side. This will limit the devil considerably, for he will attack all that he can attack. But where a hedge is built, there is little he can do.
2. He must attack the devil before the devil attacks him. He should ask the Lord to show him the plans that Satan is making against him and, when they are shown to him, he should attack the plans violently in prayer, sowing division in the devil's camp and relentlessly bringing his plans to nought.
3. He must cry to the Lord to deliver him from the evil one. Job did not seem to have done this.

If the Lord could just deliver people from the evil one without their asking, He would not have asked the saints to pray that they be delivered from the evil one. When the Lord asks people to pray, it is indicative of the fact that, unless they pray, He will not act. We have then a choice of either praying for deliverance and being delivered or not praying and having the full measure of the Enemy's blows. The choice is ours and the consequences of the choice are ours as well. Praise the Lord!

28

JESUS TAUGHT THEM THAT IT WAS NECESSARY TO BELIEVE BEFORE THEY SAW

"*On the following day, when they came from Bethany, he was hungry. And seeing in the distance a fig tree in leaf, he went to see if he could find anything on it. When he came to it, he found nothing but leaves, for it was not the season for figs. And he said to it, 'May no one ever eat from you again.' And his disciples heard it*" (Mark 11:12-14).

"*As they passed by in the morning, they saw the fig tree withered away to its roots. And Peter remembered and said to him, 'Master, look! The fig tree which you cursed has withered.' And Jesus answered them, 'Have faith in God. Truly, I say to you, whoever says to this mountain, 'Be taken up and cast into the sea,' and does not doubt in his heart, but believes that what he says will come to pass, it will be done for him. Therefore I tell you, whatever you ask in prayer, believe that you have received it and it will be yours*" (Mark 11:20-24).

OBJECTS HAVE "EARS"

When the Lord Jesus expected a tree that was in leaf to have that which ought to have accompanied the leaves fruit but it did not, He decided that such a tree that gave a false impression should no longer continue to exist. He cursed it. In cursing it, He did not pray to the Father, saying, "Father, I pray that You would cause this tree never to produce fruit again." He instead spoke directly to the tree. There are times when it is wrong to pray. The person who prays when he ought to speak to the situation is not being a man of prayer. He is being a man of lying.

The sad thing is that, too often believers who normally do not pray decide to pray when they should not. They use prayer as a way of escaping from the things that should be done. How many believers pray for the Lord to heal the sick instead of healing the sick? The command of the Lord was, "*Heal the sick*" (Luke 10:9). They went and healed the sick. They saw the sick and they spoke to the sickness in the name of Jesus and the sickness heard and obeyed. They spoke to the demons in the name of Jesus to depart and the demons departed. This was the exercise of spiritual authority

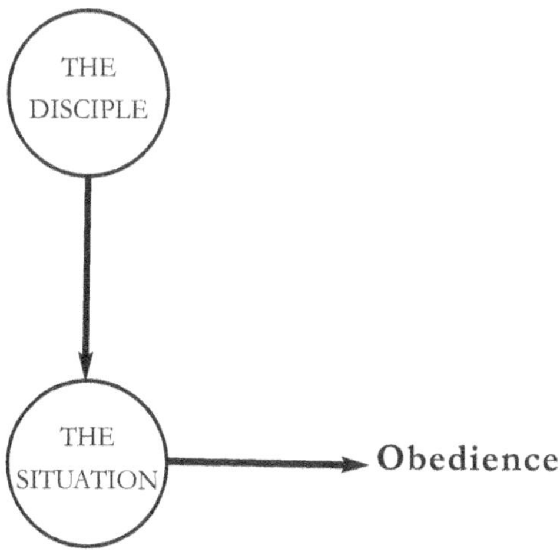

The Exercise of Authority

The Lord Jesus ministered in this way. Let us look at a few examples: "*And when he got into the boat, his disciples followed him. And behold, there arose a great storm on the sea, so that the boat was being swamped by the waves, but he was asleep. And they went and woke him, saying, 'Save us, Lord, we are perishing.' And he said to them, 'Why are you afraid, O men of little faith?' Then he rose and rebuked the winds and the sea; and there was a great calm. And the men marvelled, saying, 'What sort of man is this, that even winds and sea obey him?'* " (Matthew 8:23-27).

"*And in the synagogue there was a man who had the spirit of an un-*

clean demon; and he cried out with a loud voice, 'Ah! What have you to do with us, Jesus of Nazareth? Have you come to destroy us? I know who you are, the Holy One of God.' But Jesus rebuked him, saying, 'Be silent, and come out of him!' And when the demon had thrown him down in the midst, he came out of him having done him no harm. And they were amazed and said to one another, 'What is this word? For with authority and power he commands the unclean spirits and they come out' " (Luke 4:33-36).

"*And he arose and left the synagogue and entered Simon's house. Now Simon's mother-in-law was ill with a high fever, and they besought him for her. And he stood over her and rebuked the fever and it left her; and immediately she rose and served them*" (Luke 4:38-39).

The Lord spent many hours with the Father in private but when He came to the public and there were challenges He spoke to the situation and there was obedience.

The Lord spoke to the storm as if the storm had ears. He spoke to the fever as if the fever had ears. Do storms and fevers have ears? The real answer is that they do not. However, behind every fever, storm, situation, are satanic spirits at work to execute the will of their master. They bring the fever and keep it there. When they are rebuked, they depart, and that is the end of the fever. There is constant warfare going on in the unseen realm. The decisions of people are determined either by the wicked spirits pressurizing them or by the influence of the Holy Spirit and God's angels who labour to impose the will of God. We shall come to this in another chapter.

Because "fevers", "winds", "rivers", "roads", and so forth have "ears" they should be spoken to. Those who believe that God will back them and impose obedience upon these "objects" or these "situations" have faith and as they speak out, it happens. They, therefore, speak and it happens.

FAITH AND PRAYER

Prayer includes a reception of the will of God in the inner man and a prayer of that will back to God, so that God may execute it.

In prayer, a man receives that which God wants done. He then prays it back to God, thus fulfilling his role as God's co-worker. When God receives the desire that was originally on His heart now coming back to Him as the prayer of man, His heart rejoices and He acts both to satisfy His own heart and the heart of man, by granting the request. He then carries out divine action and behold, it happens!

It requires faith to receive divine revelation and believe it. It requires faith to believe that God will answer prayer. Where there is much faith, there is much revelation. Where there is little faith, there is little revelation. Where there is no faith, there is no revelation. Where there is much revelation, there will be much praying. When there is limited revelation, there will be limited praying and when there is no revelation, there is no praying.

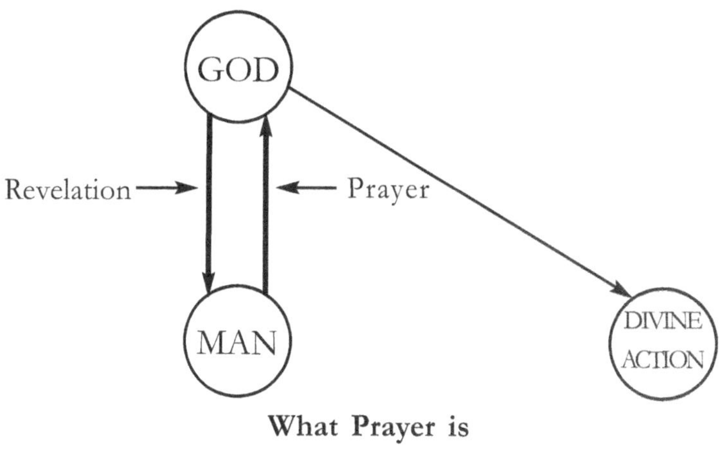

What Prayer is

The praying is proportional to the revelation and the revelation is proportional to the faith. Therefore the praying is proportional to the faith of the one who prays.

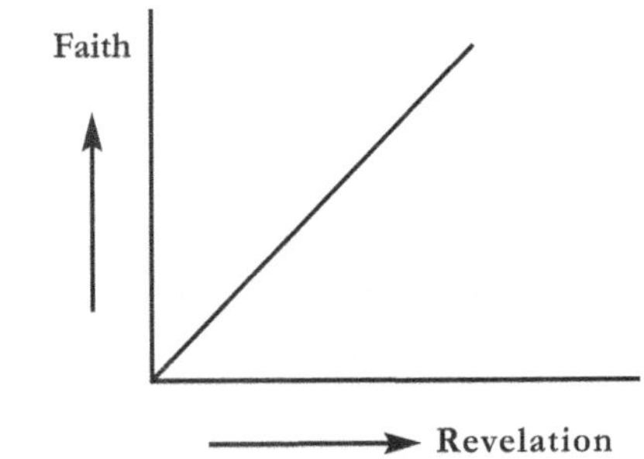

The Relationship between Revelation and Faith

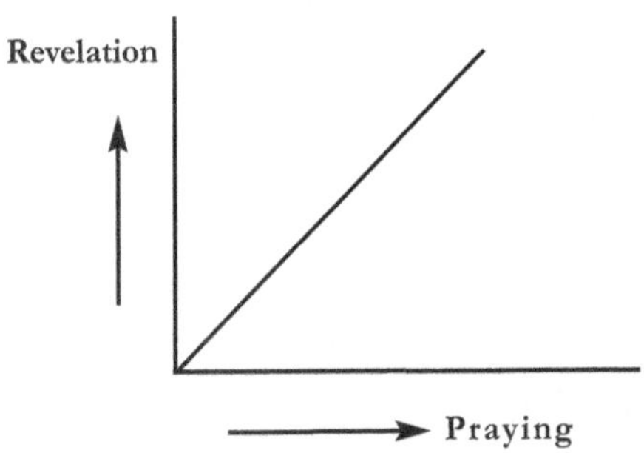

The Relationship between Revelation and Praying

GOD PLACES PREMIUM VALUE ON FAITH

The Bible sys, "*And without faith it is impossible to please him. For whosoever would draw near to God must believe that he exists and that he rewards those who seek him*" (Hebrews 11:6).

Prayer is drawing near to God. For anyone to draw near without firm assurance that he is drawing near to an existing, living, hearing and responding God, is to waste time. For anyone to draw near without full assurance that He rewards those who diligently seek Him, is to waste time.

The price to be paid in prayer is so high that only those who believe that God will surely hear and act, can continue at it. Those who occasionally throw in a sentence or two at God as a routine or in time of crisis, are not really praying. It does not require faith to do that. However, to put all else aside and make wrestling with God a way of life for one, two, three or four hours everyday, is serious business. It requires faith in God to do that and keep doing it throughout one's life.

The Lord dealt with people according to their faith. A few examples from the Word will illustrate this carefully:

1. "*Jesus turned, and seeing her, he said, 'Take heart, daughter, your faith has made you well.' And instantly the woman was made well!*" (Matthew 9:22).
2. "*When he entered the house the blind men came to him; and Jesus said to them, 'Do you believe that I am able to do this?' They said to him, 'Yes, Lord.' Then he touched their eyes, saying, 'According to your faith be it done to you.' And their eyes were opened. And Jesus sternly charged them, 'See that no one knows it'*" (Matthew 9:28-30).

If God places premium value on faith and if faith is indispensable to the prayer life, then it becomes important to know what faith is. The Bible says, "*Now, faith is the assurance of things hoped for, the conviction (evidence) of things not seen*" (Hebrews 11:1).

So faith has to do with the now. Hope has to do with the future. A student may say, "I hope to do well in my examination." That is hope. It is not faith. Hope is the glad expectation of good. Hope says "Good is coming to me." Hope is expecting good in the future. Faith is saying that that good, which is expected in the future, is mine now! The student who has faith does not say, "I will pass my examination," but "I have passed my examination. The results will be published tomorrow." He knows now what the results that will be published tomorrow are and he speaks them aloud.

The person who has faith prays that the Lord should heal him. When he has finished praying, he knows that the Lord has healed him and he puts aside his blanket, gets out of bed and begins to do the things that he was doing before he fell sick, regardless of what the symptoms are in his body. As he continues that way, thus acting out his faith, the symptoms disappear completely.

So the person believed that the Lord would heal him when he touched Him in prayer. From the moment he touched the Lord in prayer He knew that he was healed. Knowing (without outward evidence) that he was healed, he acted upon the knowledge, got up and began to do things as before and the faith was manifested. This knowing without outward evidence is what is called revelation and this acting upon revelation is the action of faith.

That is why the Lord Jesus said, "Whatever you ask in prayer, believe that you have received it and it will be yours." So there are three things:

1. Ask in prayer.
2. Have faith that you have received.
3. Have what you have received.

The first thing is to ask clearly. After asking, the natural mind would say, wait and see. If you receive what you asked, you will then believe that it is yours. However, the Lord, operating at the level of faith, said, "Ask, believe that you have received and, afterwards, you will see what you already received." That means that the receiving comes before the seeing.

The thing that will distinguish the person operating at the natural level from the one who is operating by faith is when the confession comes in the natural person will:

1. ask,
2. receive,
3. see what he has received,
4. confess that he has received it.

The person of faith will :

1. ask,
2. receive by faith,
3. confess that he has received even though what he has received is not yet visible to sight,
4. see (with the eyes) that which was received.

The man of faith confesses that he has received before he sees with the eyes. The man without faith confesses that he has received after he sees with the eyes. The man without faith runs no risk. He does not stake anything. The man of faith runs a risk. He stakes everything on God's faithfulness. He reasons that, if God has promised and is faithful, then His promises are as real as actual acts. He, therefore, counts the promises of God not just as words but as things. The promise of God to heal is taken for actual healing and actual health. The promise of God to supply funds is taken as money already received. This is faith.

It becomes evident that for the person who walks by faith there are two "seeing"s. There is the inner "seeing" through the eyes of faith and there is the outer "seeing" through the physical eyes. The person of faith moves according to what he sees with the eyes of faith. He does not move according to his feelings or according to his reasoning. He moves according to what he "sees" in his inner man. He "sees" the answer of God as having been given (in the inner man) and then confesses with his mouth what has been seen "inside." As he thus confesses, that which was "seen", "inside" is exteriorized for the physical eyes to now see.

Without this inward "seeing," the confession of faith becomes guesswork and is bound to lead to failure.

This means that a person actually only confesses the things that he asks and sees inwardly that he has received them. What he asks but does not see inwardly to have received, he must not confess that he has received; for that will be a false confession and it will lead to nothing. We can actually say that people only confess what they see. The man of faith confesses what he sees inwardly as having been received, while the man without faith confesses what he sees (outwardly) as having been received.

We have said that faith is based on the promises of God. There are two types of promises of God. There are the promises of God given in the Bible and there are the promises of God given to individuals on a day-to-day basis.

Actually, the two are one; for the promises of God that are made to His children on a day-to-day basis at a private level, are the application by the Holy Spirit to individual believers of those promises that are made to all believers in the Bible.

For example, God has promised to protect His children. That is a general promise which He has made repeatedly in many parts of Scripture. When a believer is praying for protection today, the Holy Spirit may take one of those promises in the Bible and "give" it to that believer personally in a given situation. The believer now has a personal revelation, an inner "seeing" of what God has given. He then confesses it and then finds that in the most dangerous situation, he has been kept unharmed.

A VITAL UNION WITH THE LORD IS NECESSARY

As I write this I am compelled in a new way to see the fact that there is no substitute for a close walk with the Lord for anyone who wants to really pray. Faith is closely related to revelation and revelation is inseparable from a very close walk with the Lord. How will anyone who is not walking close to the Lord have the revelation that results in "inner seeing?"

Another thing I see is that there is no substitute for much time spent in the presence of God. It is those who spend much time in His presence, who will receive a revelation of what His need is. As they receive the revelation, they will begin to pray according to His will. As they pray according to His will, they will receive inward revelation that what they are asking has been granted. As they thus receive the revelation, they will confess it and afterwards see it pass into realization.

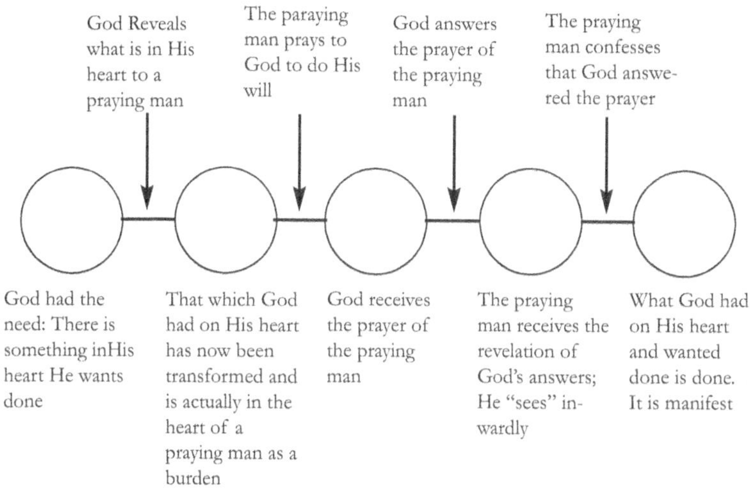

This whole process will fail if there is no faith, for without faith God's needs cannot be known, prayer is impossible, God answering prayer is impossible, the assurance that God has answered before the answer has been made visible, is impossible.

THE RELATIONSHIP BETWEEN GOD'S NEEDS,PRAYER AND FAITH

My one suggestion to all who want to know God and grow in prayer, is that they should draw near to God and establish vital fellowship with Him. They should labour to stay in His presence, never going away from there. In that way they will know him, know His needs, know how to talk to Him, know how to "receive and see" in the inner man, and then satisfy God. We shall develop this theme more fully and discuss the mechanisms of faith in our book, ***The Phenomenon of Prayer***.

29

JESUS TAUGHT THEM TO PRAY IN HIS NAME

"*You did not choose me, but I chose you and appointed you that you should go and bear fruit and that your fruit should abide; so that whatever you ask the Father in my name, he may give it to you*" (John 15:16).

"*Do you not believe that I am in the Father and the Father in me? The words that I say to you I do not speak on my own authority; but the Father who dwells in me does his works. Believe me that I am in the Father and the Father in Me; or else believe me for the sake of the works themselves. Truly, truly, I say to you, he who believes in me will also do the works that I do; and greater works than these will he do because I go to the Father. Whatever you ask in my name, I will do it, that the Father may be glorified in the Son; if you ask anything in my name, I will do it*" (John 14:10-14).

"*In that day you will ask nothing of me. Truly, truly; I say to you, if you ask anything of the Father, he will give it to you in my name. Hitherto you have asked nothing in my name; ask, and you will receive, that your joy may be full. I have said this to you in figures; the hour is coming when I shall no longer speak to you in figures but tell you plainly of the Father. In that day you will ask in my name; and I do not say to you that I shall pray the Father for you; for the Father himself loves you, because you have loved me and have believed that I came from the Father*" (John 16:23-27).

THE NAME OF JESUS IS NOT A CHARM

Very often believers treat the name of Jesus as if it was a charm. They start or end prayer by uttering the words, "In the name of the Lord Jesus" or "In Jesus' name." Somehow, many think that because they have added that statement to their prayer, they are going to have a new kind of power and receive special attention. It is very obvious that that is not what the Lord had in mind when he told the disciples to ask in His name and it would be given to them.

In John 15:16 the Lord said the following :

1. You did not choose Me.
2. I chose you.
3. I appointed you.
4. You should go and bear fruit.
5. Your fruit should abide.

SO THAT

6. Whatever you ask the Father in My name, he may give it to you.

As is seen here, asking in Jesus' name was to be done by people chosen and appointed by Him to go and bear fruit that abides. They were to bear fruit that abided, so that whatever they asked in His name would be given them by the Father. Asking in the name of the Lord Jesus was to be done by people who met specific requirements in relationship and ministry to Him. Such people were people who knew Him so well and were committed to Him so deeply that the fruit they bore would abide. They were people whose "whatever" would not include anything that the Lord would not have asked. They were to be people who would ask only what He would ask; and they would ask it in the timing that He would have asked it; they would ask it for the motives for which He would have asked. In short, they would be His mouthpiece in asking.

In John 14:10-14, the Lord said the following:

1. They were to believe that He was in the Father and the Father in Him.
2. The words that He spoke to them were not spoken on His own authority but on the Father's authority.
3. The one who believed in Him would do the works He did.
4. The one who believed in Him would do greater works than He did because He was going to the Father.
5. Because He was going to the Father, whatever they asked in His name He would do it.
6. He would do it so that the Father should be glorified in the Son.
7. If they asked anything in His name, He would do it.

Again those who could ask anything in the name of Jesus and it would be done for them had to meet specific requirements. They were to believe that the Son was in the Father and the Father in the Son. They were to see clearly that He was not acting on His own authority but on His Father's own authority. Acting thus, not on their own authority but on His authority, they were to ask whatever they wanted in His name and He would do it for them so that the Father should be glorified in the Son.

We see clearly that those who were to ask in His name were people who were vitally related to Him, people under His authority and acting under His authority. They were people who, because they were under His authority, would only ask what He wanted asked, for the purpose He wanted them to ask it for, and the way He wanted them to ask for it. They were people who would ask things with only one goal in mind: that the Father might be glorified in the Son. Such people would, consequently, never dare to ask anything that the Lord Jesus would not have asked or ask anything that the Lord Jesus is not asking. They would not ask anything for any other reason except to have the Father glorified in the Son. So, who they were, what they asked and why they asked it, was such that it was impossible for them not to receive what they asked. They asked what Jesus was asking, in the way in which Jesus was asking it and for the reason for which Jesus would have asked it. Asking in this way, they were sure to receive.

In John 16:23-27, the Lord was saying the following:

1. If they asked anything of the Father, He would give it to them in His (Jesus') name.
2. They had hitherto asked nothing in His name.
3. They were to ask and they would receive.
4. They were to ask and receive; so that their joy might be full.
5. In the future they would ask in His name.
6. In the future He would not need to pray the Father for them.
7. The Father Himself loves them.
8. They have loved Jesus and
9. They have believed that Jesus came from the Father.

Again we find that it was not just anyone who would ask anything in the name of Jesus and it would be done for him. It is the one who is loved of the Father, because that one loves Jesus and believes that Jesus came from the Father. The one who loves Jesus believes that Jesus came from the Father and also knows that Jesus did not do His will but always sought and did the Father's will. Consequently, those who were to ask in the name of Jesus would put the will of Jesus as the only one to be done and put aside their own wills completely. In thus emptying themselves of their own wills and committing themselves without reservation to His will, they would ask whatsoever they wanted in His name and it would be granted them. However, by virtue of relationship to the Lord Jesus, they would always ask what He wanted asked. They would ask it the way He wanted it asked and they would ask it for the purpose for which He wanted it that the Father might be glorified in the Son and the Son in the Father.

WHAT THEN IS ASKING IN THE NAME OF JESUS?

Asking in the name of Jesus is asking by people who know Jesus, who love Him and who are irrevocably committed to Him. Such people ask what Jesus would have asked and they ask what Jesus is asking. They ask in the way in which Jesus asked and in the way in which Jesus is asking. They ask for the purpose for which Jesus asked and for the purpose for which Jesus is asking the glory of the Father.

Those who ask in the name of Jesus ensure that there is nothing in their lives that would displease Jesus, even one bit, nor in any way stand in His way. They ensure that they are paying the price in prayer that He paid and thus asking as He asked and as He is asking from the throne today. They ensure that they have been delivered from self and have only one reason for asking the reason that Jesus had for asking (which is also the reason which He has for asking today from the throne). That reason is that the Father might be glorified in the Son.

People who meet these requirements and pray this way, are asking in the name of Jesus whether or not they use the phrase, "In Jesus' name."

Those who are unconsecrated, are divided in heart; they still abide in or practise sin, still love the world and want the world's goods and the world's possessions, are covetous and earthly minded, are filled with all manner of selfish desires and selfish motives, cannot pray in the name of the Lord Jesus. They do not pray in the name of the Lord Jesus, even though they may use those words.

PRAYER IS THE WORK OF THE CONSECRATED

It is increasingly clear that real prayer is the work of people who have been delivered from sin and self, the love of the world and the love of the things that are in the world. It is an activity of people who have learnt to pray from the Lord Jesus and whose one purpose of living is the glory of the Father. That purpose fills their lives and all that they are and all that they do, including their praying.

For such people, all their lives are lived in the name of Jesus and all their activities are carried out in the name of Jesus and for the glory of the Father. They cannot dissociate prayer from the rest of their lives, since it has become the very air they breathe and the very best method by which they do everything.

The Lord calls all His own to be like this. Make sure you answer His call promptly. The day for doing so is today!

30

JESUS TAUGHT THEM THE INDISPENSABLE HUMILITY

"*He also told this parable to some who trusted in themselves that they were righteous and despised others: 'Two men went up into the temple to pray, one a Pharisee and the other a tax collector. The Pharisee stood and prayed thus with himself, 'God, I thank thee that I am not like other men, extortioners, unjust, adulterers, or even like this tax collector. I fast twice a week; I give tithes of all that I get.' But the tax collector, standing far off would not even lift up his eyes to heaven, but beat his breast, saying, 'God, be merciful to me a sinner!' I tell you, this man went down to his house justified rather than the other; for everyone who exalts himself will be humbled, but he who humbles himself will be exalted'* " (Luke 18:9-14).

THE PHARISEE AT PRAYER

The Lord told the parable of these two men who went into the temple to pray. The people prayed according to what they were. A man always prays according to what his heart is like.

The Pharisee stood. His posture was one of arrogance. He knew nothing from the heart about the greatness of God. He knew no awe. All was the attitude of someone who was talking to an equal.

The Pharisee prayed to himself. He was not tuned to God.

He did not bother as to whether or not God was hearing him. He was satisfied to be talking. What he said came back to his ears and made him feel important. His prayers left his mouth, bounced on the ceiling and came back to him, and he received them gladly.

He addressed the eternal Father rudely; for he said, "God…" Then he plunged into an exhibition of self. This exhibition of self was immediately manifested in the many "I's" that characterized his prayer to himself.

I thank thee.

I am not like other men.

I am not an extortioner.

I am not unjust.

I am not an adulterer.

I am not like this tax collector.

I fast twice a week.

I give tithes of all that I get.

There was no room whatever for God in his prayer to himself. He just told God how wonderful he was and how well he had done everything. He had nothing to ask the Lord to do for him. He had done everything and done it so well. He had nothing to thank the Lord for. After all, God had done nothing and he had done everything. He expected God to congratulate him and clap for him. He was so blind that he could not see anything wrong in his attitude. He was oblivious of his self-righteousness. As far as he was concerned, there were only four sins that could be committed: extortion, injustice, adultery, tax collecting. According to him there were two acts of righteousness that had to be committed fasting twice a week and tithing. He did not see that there could be another sin. He could not see that there was more to do beyond fasting twice a week and tithing his income. He had set his own standards of righteousness and fulfilled them and felt very good about it. He despised others. He said that he was not like the others. He was a judge who put all the others on a balance and found them wanting. He alone was righteous. He looked with contempt at the publican who came to pray. He spoke against him to the Lord.

THE PHARISEE OF TODAY

When I read what the Pharisee said, I have to confess that I know one other Pharisee apart from the Pharisee mentioned in the passage. That Pharisee is me. I am very much like him. It is not that I say the things that he said in my prayers to the Lord, but that I often utter them daily. I often say that the unbelievers are dishonest, false, corrupt, liars and so on. I do not say that I am not like them but as I list their failures, it can hardly be misunderstood that I am saying that I thank God that I am not like them. I have to acknowledge that I even compare myself favourably against some believers, as if to say, "I thank God that I am not like them." I see this to be the spirit of the Pharisee. Lord, I am a Pharisee in attitude. Lord, have mercy upon me. Lord, have mercy upon me.

I see another aspect of the character of the Pharisee in my heart. I find that to some degree, I delight in talking about what I have done for the Lord, or about what the Lord has done in me and through me. This, too, is the spirit or attitude of the Pharisee. "Lord, have mercy on me. The very fact that I delight to talk about my successes and rarely talk about my failures, exposes me for the Pharisee that I am. Lord, have mercy upon me. Lord, have mercy upon me. Lord deliver me from the rudiments of the self-like and cause Your blessings to fall upon me. I need You, O Lord my God. My Lord, I need You. Have mercy on me, O Lord, my God.

"You said that the one who exalts himself will be humbled. I have often exalted myself. I deserve to be humbled. How mighty has Your grace been to me, Lord! You have shown abundant mercy towards me. Receive praise, honour and majesty. Help me, Lord, to begin to exalt You and to begin to exalt others. Lord, help me to begin to put others first and myself next, after You have been given the very best place. Lord, do it; for I ask in the name of the Lord Jesus.

"Lord, change me fundamentally so that my preoccupation should be the glory of Your name, the glory of the names of others and only lastly will I seek my own interest. Lord, work this out in me. The Lord Jesus lived for You and lived for others. He was totally given to others. Lord, let the same life be produced in me from day to day. Lord, let it be; for I ask in the name of the Lord Jesus."

THE TAX COLLECTOR AT PRAYER

As we have seen, the Pharisee went to pray. He prayed to himself and left the place with no touch of God whatsoever. He went in full of himself and came out even fuller of himself. He had accomplished nothing except to invite the Lord to bring him down from his high horse.

The tax collector also went to pray. He had no personal merit to boast of. He had no dead works to boast of. He was so conscious of his own unworthiness that he could not compare himself to anyone. He considered himself to be the very last; all he did was to stand in humility afar off and cry out to God. Unlike the Pharisee who prayed with himself and to himself, the tax collector prayed to God. He said to God, "Be merciful to me a sinner." He did not talk about the other sinners. He was too unworthy to talk about them. He did not compare himself to the other sinners. He knew that even if he was less sinful than other sinners, he still stood condemned because of his sin. He knew that the Lord did not weigh one sinner against another and then say, "This is the best of the sinners. He has sinned less horribly than the other sinners." He knew that the Word of the Lord said that if a person keeps the whole law but fails in one thing, he has become guilty of the whole law. He knew that even if he had not extorted, committed injustice, committed adultery or any such sins, the very fact that he did not love the Lord as he ought to already condemned him. He knew that it was useless to talk about what he had done, whereas the things that he had not done were clearly before him. His eyes were open. He saw himself and he saw the Lord. He pleaded with the Lord for mercy. He came in humility. He came as if to the Cross and pleaded there, "Lord, have mercy upon me, sinner that I am." God must have heard him. God heard him. God forgave him. He went away forgiven, justified and exalted. The Lord always does that to those who come with broken and contrite hearts.

THE INDISPENSABLE HUMILITY

The Lord has reserved His best for the humble and for the meek. He says in His Word, "*For every one who exalts himself will be humbled, and he who humbles himself will be exalted*" (Luke 14:11). "*The reward for humility and fear of the Lord is riches and honour and life*" (Proverbs 22:4). "*Before destruction a man's heart is haughty, but humility goes before honour*" (Proverbs 18:12).

The Lord looks with favour on the humble. He resists the proud of heart. Since prayer is essentially carried out in the presence of the Lord, the proud of heart offend Him. They cannot even be allowed to establish contact with Him, because from the word go, they are displeasing to Him. He will not even listen to them. Nothing that the proud of heart say can please God in any way.

When Nebuchadnezzar spoke in pride, the Lord dealt with him. The Bible says, "*At the end of twelve months he was walking on the roof of the royal palace of Babylon, and the king said, 'Is not this great Babylon, which I have built by my mighty power as a royal residence for the glory of my majesty?' While the words were still in the king's mouth, there fell a voice from heaven, 'O King Nebuchadnezzar, to you it is spoken: The kingdom has departed from you, and you shall be driven from among men, and your dwelling shall be with the beast of the field; and you shall be made to eat grass like an ox; and seven times shall pass over you, until you have learned that the Most High rules the kingdom of men and gives it to whom he will'*" (Daniel 4:29-32).

God brought down Nebuchadnezzar because of his pride, but

when he learnt humility, God exalted him. He said, "*At the end of the days I, Nebuchadnezzar, lifted my eyes to heaven, and my reason returned to me, and I blessed the Most High, and praised and honoured him who lives for ever; for his dominion is an everlasting dominion, and his kingdom endures from generation to generation; all the inhabitants of the earth are accounted as nothing; and he does according to his will in the host of heaven and among the inhabitants of the earth; and none can stay his hand or say to him, 'What doest thou?' At the same time my reason returned to me; and for the glory of my kingdom, my majesty and splendour returned to me. My counsellors and my lords sought me, and I was established in my kingdom, and still more greatness was added to me. Now I, Nebuchadnezzar, praise and extol and honour the king of heaven; for all his works are right and his ways are just; and those who walk in pride he is able to abase*" (Daniel 4:34-37).

THE LORD JESUS WAS HUMBLE

The Lord Jesus had every reason to exalt Himself. First of all, He was already exalted. Secondly, He could exalt Himself and no one would bring Him down. However, He did not exalt Himself. "*He did not count equality with God a thing to be grasped. He emptied himself, taking the form of a servant, being born in the likeness of men. And being found in human form he humbled himself and became obedient unto death, even death on a cross. Therefore God has highly exalted him and bestowed on him the name which is above every name, that at the name of Jesus every knee should bow, in heaven and on earth and under the earth, and every tongue confess that Jesus Christ is Lord, to the glory of God the Father*" (Philippians 2:6-11).

He invites His disciples to learn from Him. "*Take my yoke upon you, and learn from me; for I am gentle and lowly in heart, and you will find rest for your souls*" (Matthew 11:29).

HUMILITY AND PRAYER

We have said that the proud of heart have no place before the God of heaven. He resists them and abases them. However, there are people who have begun to learn humility. How is humility related to prayer? We say without doubt that the prayers of the more humble are more powerful. Impact is proportional to the degree of humility that has been attained by the one praying. The greater the humility, the greater the impact and the lesser the humility, the lesser the impact. We can illustrate it as follows:

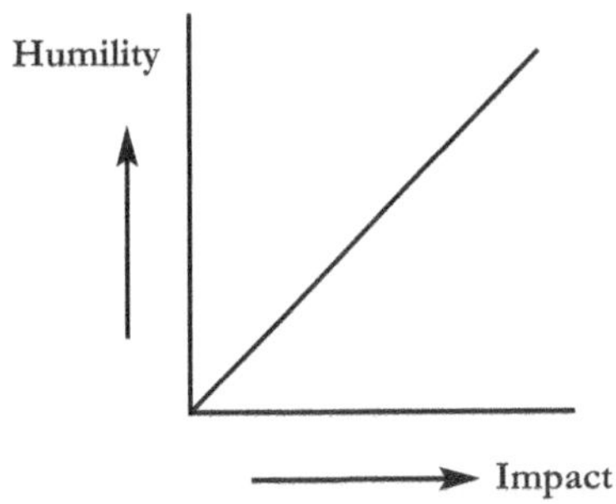

The Reletionship between Humility and Impact

The prayers of the proud have little impact.

THE SCHOOL OF HUMILITY

Because humility has such great bearing on the prayer life, those who want to make progress in the Ministry of Prayer should enrol in The School of Humility and make progress there. Such should remain students in The School of Humility; for as long as they are in the Ministry of Prayer. In this way, as they make progress in humility, they will also make progress in the ministry of praying.

"Lord, I enrol in the School of Humility. Keep me learning in that School. Do not allow me to commit the folly of running away from it. Keep me there until the Lord Jesus comes, for I must remain in the Ministry of Praying until He comes. Amen."

Is that not also the prayer of your own heart? If it is, then insist that the Lord should take you seriously and that He should answer you. He will do so and you shall be blessed. Praise the Lord!

PART 3

THE PRAYER MINISTRY OF JESUS (2)

31

FOUR DAYS IN INTERCESSION

"Now a certain man was ill, Lazarus of Bethany, the village of Mary and her sister Martha. It was Mary who anointed the Lord with ointment and wiped his feet with her hair, whose brother Lazarus was ill. So the sisters sent to him, saying, 'Lord, he whom you love is ill.' But when Jesus heard it he said, 'This illness is not unto death; it is for the glory of God, so that the Son of God may be glorified by means of it.'

Now Jesus loved Martha and her sister and Lazarus. So when he heard that he was ill, he stayed two days longer in the place where he was. Then after this he said to his disciples, 'Let us go into Judea again.' The disciples said to him, 'Rabbi, the Jews were but now seeking to stone you, and are you going there again?' Jesus answered, 'Are there not twelve hours in the day? If anyone walks in the day, he does not stumble, because he sees the light of this world. But if anyone walks in the night, he stumbles, because the light is not in him.' Thus he spoke, and then he said to them, 'Our friend Lazarus has fallen asleep, but I go to awake him out of sleep.' The disciples said to him, 'Lord, if he has fallen asleep, he will recover.' Now Jesus had spoken of his death, but they thought that he meant taking rest in sleep. Then Jesus told them plainly, 'Lazarus is dead; and for your sake I am glad that I was not there, so that you may believe. But let us go to him.' Thomas, called the twin, said to his fellow disciples, 'Let us also go, that we may die with him'" (John 11:1-16).

Lazarus was sick and word was sent to the Lord Jesus. He did notrush to heal the sick man. Afterwards Lazarus died. Even though no one told the Lord, He knew that Lazarus was dead. He could have rushed to the place where Lazarus was and resurrected him as soon as possible. However, the Lord did not do that. He tarried for many days, so that by the time He got to Bethany, Lazarus had already been in the tomb for four days.

Why did the Lord not go immediately He heard that Lazarus was ill? Why did He not rush there as soon as He knew that he was dead? Was He just trying to delay so that He would create sensation when He got there four days after the man was dead? Was He waiting for Lazarus to be four days in the grave so that the miracle that would result from his being raised from the dead would bring greater glory to the Father? I do not think any of these was the reason why He waited for four days before He got to Bethany.

When the Lord got to Bethany, He performed a very mighty miracle and Lazarus was brought back to life. What was He doing for four or more days from the time He heard that he was sick to the time that He got there four days after the burial?

JESUS WAS FINDING OUT THE FATHER'S WILL

When the Lord heard that Lazarus was ill, He and His disciples stayed two more days longer in the place where they were before He announced that they had to go to Judea. These were two days of seeking God's will. He knew from the very moment He was told of the illness that, that illness was not unto death but that it was for the glory of God; so that the Son of God might be glorified by it.

Although He knew that, there was yet more to know before He moved to the scene of the event. He must have spent the time in prayer to His Father. We know that He always did the Father's will. We also know that He only went where His Father sent Him. So, there He was. A beloved friend was sick, dead. Beloved friends of His had sent for Him. A miracle was needed in order to restore things to normal. Such a miracle would bring glory to the Father. Should He not just move at once?

Jesus did not move according to what the situation demanded.

He did not move because He loved Lazarus. He did not move because He loved Martha and Mary and they had sent for Him. He did not move because there was an opportunity to perform a miracle and so bring glory to God. Jesus did not move because of any of these reasons; if He did, He would have moved in His own will. He would have acted independently. He would have sinned and all would have been lost for ever.

Jesus spent the time listening to His Father. He must have sought His Father and asked Him, ‘My Father, Lazarus is sick, dead. I love him. I love Martha and Mary and they have sent for Me. Lord, what do You say? I want to do Your will. I want to do only Your will. What did You ordain for Me to do from the foundation of the world? Show it to Me and I will do it. My Father, show Me Your will and I will do it. I will do it and I will do only it. Nothing else interests Me except Your will.”

When the Lord thus prayed, the Father must have shown Him that it was His perfect will for Him to go to Bethany. That settled it.

Those who will know the full glory of God are those who have resolutely put aside all that is natural natural affection, natural relationships, the demands of friends, the opportunities to do great things for God, and so on. Having put all these aside, they commit themselves to God’s will and to God’s will alone. They seek that will and they do it. If that will leads them to greatness, they accept the greatness with joy. If that will leads them to apparent failure before men, they accept that will with joy and accept the apparent failure with joy. If that will strengthens their relationships with loved ones, they accept it with joy. If that will causes loved ones to become offended and to withdraw, they accept it with joy. They have found their joy in doing the Father’s will. They are committed to it and nothing can be allowed to tamper with that.

That is the pathway of greatness before the Lord. The Lord calls all who are His to it. Let us separate ourselves completely from every other tie and be welded to Him and to His will, and then we shall fully satisfy His heart.

JESUS WAS SEEING THE NEEDED ANOINTING

It is presumption to think that because God has called us to do something for His glory, we can move anyhow to the site of action and the thing will be done. It is presumption to think that all that is required of us is that we should seek the Lord, know Him and obey Him and everything will be wonderful. Only an unwise person receives a task from the Lord and rushes there without receiving from Him the needed power for its accomplishment.

The Lord told the apostles, "*Thus it is written, that the Christ should suffer and so on the third day rise from the dead, and that repentance and forgiveness of sins should be preached in his name to all nations, beginning from Jerusalem. You are witnesses of these things*" (Luke 24:46-48). Had it been all He said, they would have gone on to a tragedy; for they would have had no power to do the work. He added, "*And behold I send the promise of my Father upon you, but stay in the city, until you are clothed with power from on high*" (Luke 24:49). They obeyed, stayed in the city until they were clothed with power from on high.

The Word of God says, "*Seek the Lord and his strength, seek his presence continually*" (Psalm 105:4). It is not a call to seek the Lord only. The call is to seek the Lord, seek the Lord's strength and seek the Lord's presence. Those who are obedient seek the Lord and find Him. They seek His strength and receive it and they seek His presence and are lost in it.

It was said of Stephen that he was full of :

1. The Spirit of wisdom (Acts 6:3).
2. Faith and the Holy Spirit (Acts 6:5).
3. Grace and power (Acts 6:8).

He could have been full of the spirit of wisdom but not of

faith and of the Holy Spirit. He could have been full of faith and the Holy Spirit and not of grace and power. If he were full only of the spirit of wisdom, faith, the Holy Spirit and grace, it is possible that he might not have performed any miracles. However, the Bible says, "*And Stephen, full of grace and power, did great wonders and signs among the people*" (Act 6:8). The signs and great wonders happened because he was full of power and not simply because he was full of the Holy Spirit. Barnabas is the other person (apart from the Lord Jesus) who was full of the Holy Spirit and faith (Acts 11:24) but did not perform any signs and wonders, although he was of outstanding spirituality and ministry.

As the Lord Jesus ministered, power left Him. He needed constantly to be refilled. It is probable that He spent the time between the time He heard of Lazarus' death and the time He appeared on the scene seeking a fresh anointing from the Father to replenish that which had been used up in ministry.

Finally, I think that He spent time in intercession. How He must have pleaded with the Father that the Father should allow Lazarus to be brought back to life. How He must have pleaded that the Father should cause His will to be accomplished. How He refused to take for granted that the Father would automatically work to bring His will to execution! It was a battle with the Father in mighty intercession and pleading and, after four days, He won the battle before His Father. After He won the battle in the secret place of prayer and intercession, He moved to the site of action and prayed a prayer of thanksgiving that might have taken just one minute or so: "*Father, I thank thee that thou hast heard me. I knew that thou hearest me always, but I have said this on account of the people standing by, that they may believe that thou didst send me*" (John 11:41-42).

It was so simple. In fact, it was a prayer mainly for testimony. Many heard that prayer and perhaps thought that that was all the praying that it took. The Father heard that prayer and knew that it was the sealing of four days of arduous battle, and that He was confessing before man the things that were settled at the warfront before Him. The Father heard it and rejoiced and made the Son more than equal to the task; so that when He cried out with a loud voice, "*Lazarus, come out*" (John 11:43), no power anywhere could have stopped the voice of the Son from being heard and obeyed. That voice, fully energised by the Father's power, penetrated the tomb, penetrated the land of the dead and penetrated the dead body of Lazarus, and then imparted life again to him. That voice went forth with healing power; so that Lazarus was healed, and when he came out of the grave, he was both alive and in perfect health.

May we, too, follow His example, refusing to take God for granted. May we receive our work from Him and may we refuse to presume that, because things are ordained by Him, they will simply happen because we have obeyed. May we seek His power and receive it and thus go to do His will, filled not only with the Holy Spirit, but also with the power of the Holy Spirit. May we pray and pray and pray until we have won the battle before God, and then may we go and act out before men the victory we have won in private before God: then we shall be fully blessed. Praise the Lord!

32

THE FATHER WHO ALWAYS HEARS

"*And Jesus lifted up his eyes and said, 'Father, I thank thee that thou hast heard me. I knew that thou hearest me always'*" (John 11:41-42).

The Lord Jesus was standing at the graveside of Lazarus. The man had been dead for four days. He commanded that the stone that sealed the tomb be removed. He was about to command Lazarus to come out of the tomb.

Normally, it ought to have been a tense moment. He ought to have been afraid, asking, "What will happen if my command to him to come out meets with silence and nothing happens?" The Lord did not react that way. He lifted up His eyes and said, "Father I thank Thee that thou hast heard me. I know that thou hearest me always." He prayed or rather He proclaimed aloud so that everyone might hear Him "Father, Thou hast heard Me. Father, I know that Thou hearest Me always."

FATHER, I THANK THEE THAT THOU HAST HEARD ME

The Lord Jesus was praying for the first time publicly at that occasion. Why did He thank the Father for hearing Him? When did He ask and was heard? It must be a report of what happened in the private arena of His praying. As we said in the last chapter, He must have carried out much praying in private to God. He must have wrestled through to victory. He must have asked and received in prayer in the privacy of His communion with the Father. It was secret business that was now coming to the public.

There are people whose transactions with God are all a matter of the public. They know nothing of secret dealings with Him. They know nothing of an hour, a day, a week, or a month in private with Him so that He may say something to them that remains a secret between Him and them. This is a great pity; for no one can make progress beyond the elementary, unless there are secret dealings between God and him. Let me ask you a question, "What is it that ever transpired between the Lord and you that you have not shared with anybody? Is there something in your relationship with Him, something that unites both of you, something that is precious to Him and to you, something that is too intimate, so that you just know that this must never be shared? Has He ever told you something and added, 'Please, do not tell any man this thing that I have told you'?" If there is nothing between you and the Lord that you are reluctant to share, then your relationship with Him is superficial.

May you consecrate more time to being in His presence. May you give Him increasing opportunity to enjoy your presence. As you linger increasingly in His presence, He will one day whisper something into your ear which is deeply personal and from that day your relationship with Him will pass from the ordinary to the special.

May you labour so much in prayer alone with Him that there will be an increasing number of things about which you can say to Him in private as a testimony, "Father, I thank Thee that Thou hast heard me." May you learn to deal with Him always in private first; so that when you speak in public, your word will not fall to the ground because it is rooted in honesty with God. May you decide that you will say nothing in public which you have not sorted out in private with Him. May you spend so much time with Him in private that everything you say in public will bear the marks of authenticity. Those who settle things in private with God before they speak before man, carry with them unusual authority.

The problem with too many of us is that we are not patient enough to wait until an issue is deeply settled with God before it is announced. The result is that we can say one thing today and tomorrow we are forced to contradict ourselves. Lord, forgive me for this. Do you, too, need forgiveness? If you do, ask Him for it and then go away and be different.

I KNOW THAT THOU HEAREST ME ALWAYS

It was tremendous boldness for the Lord Jesus to make the statement, "I know that thou hearest me always." In a few minutes He was going to command Lazarus to come out of the grave. If the Father always heard Him, then it would soon be obvious. If He was lying, then the truth of it would soon be made manifest. Not long from then, the Lord called out to Lazarus and he came out of the grave alive, having died four days earlier. That incident left no doubts in any man's mind about the fact that the Father always heard the Son.

When the Lord was making that statement, He was not guessing. He was stating a plain fact. He knew it. The Father knew it and soon man knew it. That was a confession indeed.

THE FATHER ALWAYS HEARS YOU?

The question we must now ask is, "Can you also say, 'Father, I know that Thou hearest me always'?" If you made that statement, would it be true? Is it backed by your past or present history? I am afraid that I can only say, "Father, I know that You hear me most of the time." I know that that confession belittles God. Lord, forgive me for being the type of son who cannot bring joy to You by confessing that You always hear him. Lord, I repent. I will do something about it. Because many believers can only say that the

Lord sometimes hears them, we need to ask, what are the qualifications of a person who can say without fear of contradiction, "I know that the Father always hears me"? We outline the following:

1. The person must be pure in heart. He must be holy. Anyone who practises sin will not always be heard.
2. The person must be delivered from the love of the world and the love of the things of the world; for if anyone loves the world, the love of the Father would be absent in him. Where the love of the Father is absent, there can be no mighty and continuous manifestations of the Father.
3. The person must know deep-seated deliverance from the "self" life. Without this deep-seated deliverance, God's will will always be blurred by the self and, without a knowledge of God's will, there can be no praying aright.
4. The person must be resolutely committed to the will of the Lord and to no other will. The Lord will move to accomplish His will and to accomplish the will of no other. The apostle wrote, "*And this is the confidence that we have in him, that if we ask anything according to his will, he hears us. And if we know that he hears us in whatever we ask, we know that we have obtained the requests made of him*" (1 John 5:14-15). One of the first prerequisites for praying about anything is to ensure that it is the will of God. Any prayers made outside the will of God will not be answered, even if they are made by a consecrated person whose heart is pure. A person can decide something of his own and make it the subject of prayer, he may then pray it for six hours every day for fifty years. If that thing is not the will of God, his many intense prayers will be to no avail. THE FIRST PREREQUISITE IN PRAYER IS TO SEEK TO KNOW GOD'S WILL ABOUT THE MATTER.
5. The person must know the secret of praying until the Lord answers. He must be able to ask and keep asking, seek and keep seeking and to knock and keep knocking until the Lord

answers. Those who are prepared to start a prayer project and then give it up, cannot become those whom the Father always hears. The full price must be paid in every way.

6. The person must pray in faith. It is possible to pray the same matter over and over without exercising any faith. Without faith it is impossible to please God. How can the one who cannot please God also be the one whom the Father always hears?
7. The person must be an absolutely consecrated man. His all must be surrendered to the Lord in a very clear and resolute way. His will must have been put aside once and for all in everything and for all time, and that consecration must be renewed every day. God must be having absolute sway, every second in the person's life.

These are seven conditions that must be fulfilled by anyone who wants to stand in the position in which he can say, "I know the Father always hears me." That is the position in which the Lord Jesus stood. That is the position that He maintained all through His life on earth. That is why the Father honoured Him so fully and so completely.

The Father will again honour those who walk the way that the Lord Jesus walked. He will allow them do the things that He did. He will allow them to do greater things than what He did. He wants to begin today. Will you give Him an opportunity to do it? Will you let Him begin with you now?

33

THE VIOLENT PRAYING OF THE LORD JESUS

"*In the days of his flesh, Jesus offered up prayers and supplications, with loud cries and tears, to him who was able to save him from death, and he was heard for his godly fear. Although he was a Son, he learned obedience through what he suffered, and being perfect he became the source of eternal salvation to all who obey him*" (Hebrews 5:7-9).

The Lord Jesus offered up prayers and supplications with loud cries and tears, to Him who was able to save Him from death.

PRAYING LEISURELY

There are times when one can pray leisurely, for example, before or after a meal, one can offer thanksgiving leisurely, saying to the Lord, "Father, thank You for this meal. Thank You for Your constant goodness to me. I am very grateful, O Lord my God." There are other times when one can pray leisurely, times when there is no special burden and no special pressure. The only problem is that for too many believers, all they know is leisurely praying. They know nothing of violence in prayer.

VIOLENCE IN PRAYER

Violence in prayer is practised by people under pressure. It is the way of praying of people with a burden. It is the praying of people who are under special stress. It is the praying of people who know that they must pray or perish.

We are told of the Lord that in the days of His flesh, He offered up prayers and supplications with loud cries and tears. It is possible that things went as follows:

1. He prayed normally.
2. He prayed with silent cries.
3. He prayed with loud cries.
4. He prayed with loud cries and tears.
5. He supplicated with loud cries and tears.

Each step was more intense and more desperate. All hung on the balance. All depended on His prayer and His supplications. He was under great stress.

What was causing the stress? It was the fear of death not just physical death, but spiritual death. There was His holy hatred for sin and there was also the fact that He had to die as a sin-Bearer. This itself was painful. To add to this was the pressure from the Enemy to destroy Him.

The Lord Jesus did not cry out of self-pity. Why did He want to be saved from death? He wanted to be saved from death (from sin) because had He not been saved, the God-head would have disintegrated. Few can fathom the risk that God took when He sent the Lord Jesus to earth. The risk was this: If the Lord Jesus had committed even one sin, He would have become a sinner and His return to the God-head would have been impossible: there would have been total disintegration, for the triune God cannot continue without one member. For this reason He prayed and He cried. He did not only pray. He supplicated. He prayed and supplicated with loud cries and tears.

To understand this, we must bear in mind that the Lord Jesus faced all His conflicts on earth as Man. He was truly Man. That is why the writer of Hebrews talks of the days of His flesh. If the Lord had faced these conflicts as God, His temptations would have been meaningless and His overcoming them could also have been meaningless. He emptied Himself of all His powers as God, learnt obedience through the things He suffered and was perfected (as Man) through suffering.

So the Father knew that He could sin. He was tempted, pressed to sin. There were moments when all of hell stood against Him in a desperate effort to make Him sin, but He did not. At such moments, and there were possibly many of them, deliverance came to Him from the Father in answer to prayers and supplications with loud cries and tears. He did not plan to pray and supplicate. He did not plan to pray and supplicate with loud cries and tears. It was not a decision taken beforehand in order to impress God or to impress anyone. It was something that came upon Him under the pressure of a desperate burden. It was the response of the moment to what He was going through.

The Bible says that He was heard for His godly fear. The godly fear of sin drove Him to cry so desperately to God. The godly fear of what would happen to the God-head made Him cry so desperately to God. The godly fear of what would happen to the purpose of God that He served made Him pray and supplicate. The godly fear of failing to do the Father's will to which He was resolutely committed, made Him cry out desperately in prayer to the only One who could change the situation the Father.

Because He cried desperately, He was heard and delivered and, because He was heard and delivered, we are in Him today, safe and secure.

VIOLENCE IN PRAYER AND GODLY FEAR TODAY

Why is it that there is so little violence in prayer today? Why is it that there are so few who pray and supplicate with loud cries and tears to the Father? The answer is largely because godly fear has disappeared from amongst the people of God. Godly fear is no longer known in many circles that call upon the name of the Crucified.

There are hardly any who truly bother about the will of God. There are hardly any for whom the will of God is an absolute must. There are hardly any who are so committed to the holiness of God that they would rather perish than allow it to be violated. There are hardly any who are so totally given to the Kingdom of God that they would rather perish than stand in the way of that Kingdom, or they would rather perish than allow some other will to be executed in their lives. The tragedy is that we live in a period when anything will do. This permissiveness means that there is nothing, after all, that is compelling. Nothing is binding and anything can be done. Because there is no godly fear, people are not radically committed to God's holiness, Kingdom and will. It does not matter to people if they occasionally sin. It does not matter that there is much sin in the Church and in the Churches.

In addition to this, true shepherds are in short supply those who like the Chief Shepherd would say, "*And for their sakes, I sanctify myself, that they also may be sanctified by the truth*" (John 17:19, NKJV).

A true shepherd will have godly fear. He will run away from every form of evil; for he knows that his sin will ruin him and ruin the flock over which the Holy Spirit has made him overseer. This love for the flock will make him struggle against sin and resist to the point of shedding blood.

He will rather die than commit any sin. As the battle not to sin rages, he will cry out to God desperately with loud cries and tears, pleading that the Lord should save him from sin. As he cries out so desperately, the Lord will hear him and he will be delivered. He will then have saved his own soul and saved his flock from ruin; for there is a sense in which a shepherd cannot fall and the flock not fall. This is what a true shepherd would do. It will be good to ask yourself the question, "Am I a true shepherd? Do I know the same fear of God? Do I know the same hatred for sin? Do I know the same cry for deliverance?"

There are others whose problem may not be sin. Their eyes have just been opened to the meaning of being lost, of people spending an eternity away in the lake of fire, seeing this they would wrestle with God for the salvation of the lost. They would wrestle night and day crying and weeping, pleading with God that He should rise in power, pour out the Holy Spirit in an unparalleled way and let millions, nay, billions of sinners be saved. Such would take no rest and give God no rest until something special has been done by the Lord on the behalf of the lost. Such would intercede, supplicate, cry, mourn and pour themselves out night and day, day after day and night after night, until the Lord has answered. They would ask and keep asking. They would seek and keep seeking. They would knock and keep knocking, until either the heavens are shattered by their knocking or God has been wearied out of His rest to arise and do something great.

This is what I pray that the Lord should do to my heart. "Lord, I plead in the name of the Lord that You should weld my heart to the lost in such an inseparable way that I will know joy only as I am praying, supplicating, with tears and loud cries, night after night and day by day, for their salvation. Lord, weld my heart to them in such a way that I will know no joy even for one minute until I have marshalled the largest army of consecrated believers that I can possibly gather, to pray for the lost. Do it now, Lord!"

The Lord Jesus was heard for His godly fear. "Lord, I am going to wrestle with You. I will put my time consciously into being in Your presence and remain in Your presence, until You have wrought in me the godly fear that I need to function properly as Your servant. Lord, that day has come. This is the day. Bind me to the altar of prayer; so that I may never be able to go away. Lord, fill me with a new love for You; so that it will be a joy to so invest my life. Glory be to You, O Lord, my God. Amen."

34

PRAYING IN GETHSEMANE

"And he came out, and went, as was his custom, to the Mount of Olives; and the disciples followed him. And when he came to the place he said to them, 'Pray that you may not enter into temptation.' And he withdrew from them about a stone's throw and knelt down and prayed, 'Father, if thou art willing, remove this cup from me; nevertheless not my will, but thine, be done.' And there appeared to him an angel from heaven, strengthening him. And being in agony he prayed more earnestly; and his sweat became like great drops of blood falling down upon the ground. And when he rose from prayer, he came to the disciples and found them sleeping for sorrow, and he said to them, 'Why do you sleep? Rise and pray that you may not enter into temptation'" (Luke 22:39-46).

The Lord Jesus knew that that night He would be arrested. There was, however, a big question on His mind. He had to do His Father's will. He had to redeem mankind. He knew that He had to suffer. He knew all this, but as the moment for it to happen drew near, He wondered if there might be some other way open and available to the Father for the salvation of man that could spare Him not only the pain of the Cross, but also the horror of bearing all the sins of all the people of all time. He was frightened and afraid as He faced the fact that He would have to be separated from His Father, that His Father would actually turn His back on Him, that their communion that had existed from all eternity past without any interruption, would be broken. He was horrified by the knowledge that if He took the cup, He would cry to the Father from the Cross and the Father would be forced by the sin that was laid upon Him to remain silent. He felt the agony that that silence would bring to Him. He also felt the knife that would go through His Father's heart as He would have to hear His voice and keep silent. (Few know what the Cross cost the Son. Fewer know anything of what it cost the Father. In reality, the Father's agony was as much as the Son's.) So the agony of being separated from His Father, the pain of having His all-holy nature carry sin, and the even greater pain of seeing the Father suffer the separation from Him, made the prayer in Gethsemane a must. It also made it a matter of greatest intensity.

In all this there were two things. There was the cup and there was the will of the Father. At that moment, the two seemed different. Because the cup and the will did not seem to be one, and because the cup was so horrible, the Lord pleaded that it might be taken away from Him.

Cups could be taken away and cups should be taken away, but immediately a person discerns the will of God, he should yield to it. The Lord Jesus asked that the cup might be taken away. He, however, never asked that the Father's will should be altered or taken away from Him. Rather, He affirmed it by the prayer, "Nevertheless not my will, but thine be done."

When the Lord knew that the cup was the Father's will for Him, He stopped praying. The Bible says, "*Then he came to the disciples and said to them, 'Are you still sleeping and taking your rest? Behold, the hour is at hand, and the Son of man is betrayed into the hands of sinners. Rise, let us be going; see, my betrayer is at hand'* " (Matthew 26:45-46). When the Lord knew that the cup and the will of the Father were one, He said, "Rise, let us be going." He was saying, "The cup is the will of My Father for Me. Rise, let us go and bring that will to pass. Rise, let us co-operate with the Father to ensure that His will is done."

WHAT GETHSEMANE DID FOR THE LORD JESUS

What did Gethsemane do for the Lord Jesus? It can be said of the Lord Jesus that He entered Gethsemane knowing that there was God's will and there was the cup that was about to come to Him. In Gethsemane, in a totally new way, He embraced the Cross, the sin and the sins of the world, the separation from the Father and the agony that was going to be the Father's. He came out of the Garden of Gethsemane ready and even desirous to die. He came to the Garden horrified by the sinfulness of sin. He went out of the Garden identified fully with sin.

THE PRAYING THAT MADE THE DIFFERENCE

We are told that the Lord Jesus prayed away from the disciples. He had gone with them to pray but He could not pray in the same place with them. There was a burden on His heart that the disciples knew nothing about. His soul was sorrowful (Mark 14:34), theirs was not. He was fully awake. They were sleepy. People who sleep during prayer are people without burdens. No one can sleep with an undischarged burden. The burden will keep him awake and compel him to press on until it is discharged.

It could be that there was no other occasion where the Lord prayed with greater intensity. He did not only pray with intensity. He prayed with greater intensity. He did not only pray with intensity. He prayed from agony. He prayed earnestly and then He prayed more earnestly. He poured out all of Himself in this seeking to know if the cup was the Father's will. He so poured out His soul that the Father was compelled to send an angel from heaven to strengthen Him. So deep, so powerful, so exhausting was His praying that His sweat became like drops of blood.

This praying was a total outpouring of Himself to God. Such praying cannot go unheard. The Father heard Him and made things clear to Him. Had He simply prayed, things would have gone wrong. There are situations when simple praying will do. There are situations where only utter praying with total pouring away of oneself will do. For such situations those who pray simple prayers will find that their prayers do not move the hand of God.

The praying saint must discern the issues involved. He must know what can be obtained by simple praying and what can only be obtained after aggressive cries, loud cries and the like. Knowing this he will pray at the appropriate level and, thereby, satisfy the heart of God.

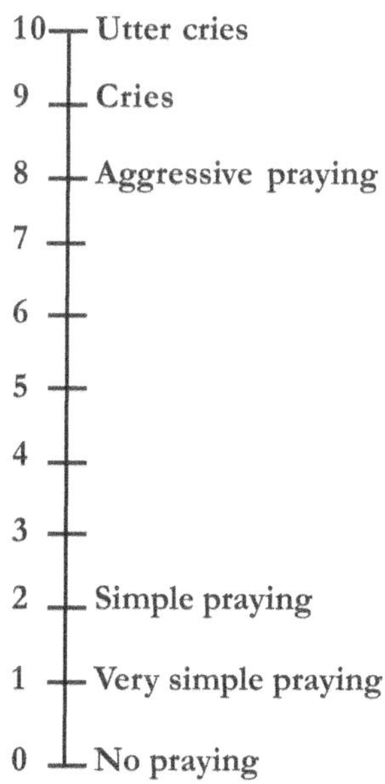

Various Levels of Intensity In Prayer

I have often asked myself what would have happened had the Lord not paid such a price in prayer in Gethsemane. I do not know, but there is one thing I am sure of: Things would have gone wrong with Him and for Him. Things would also have gone wrong for the entire world, for you and for me! Thanks be to God that He prayed as He ought to have prayed. Glory be to the Lord!

Have you ever thought about the consequence of your burden-less, easy-going prayers in the unseen realm? Think about it and do something about it. Think about it and follow the Lord's example, and then you shall be fully blessed. Amen.

35

PRAYING FROM THE CROSS

The real character of a person is manifested under stress. It is then that hidden strengths or hidden weaknesses are manifested. The Lord spoke seven sayings from the cross. These are:

1. "*Father, forgive them; for they know not what they do*" (Luke 23:34).
2. "*Truly, I say to you, today you will be with me in Paradise*" (Luke 23:43).
3. "*Woman, behold your son! Son, behold your mother*" (John 19:26-27).
4. "*My God, My God, why hast thou forsaken me?*" (Matthew 27:46).
5. "*I thirst*" (John 19:28).
6. "*It is finished*" (John 19:30).
7. "*Father, into thy hands I commit my spirit*" (Luke 23:46).

It is note-worthy that even on the cross the Lord Jesus was totally consumed by the will of the Father. Even on the cross He put the Father first, others next and Himself last. The first words from the cross had to do with the Father's will to save the lost. The second saying had to do with an offer of hope to a penitent.

The third saying had to do with the provision of a mother for His disciple and a home for His earthly mother. The priority of His speech on the cross demonstrated such utter giving up of Himself for others that it causes me to bow in utter humility.

Under the test of stress He manifested the fact that He was utterly in control. He remained spiritual, that is, moved and governed by His spirit. He did not become carnal, moved and controlled by the soul, body or environment.

Lord, I pray that You should grant me to know the same degree of self-control. Lord, grant that in an increasing way I should grow into a spiritual man, being led and being controlled by Your Spirit working on my spirit, rather than by my soul, body or the environment. Lord, I see this as crucial to a life of prayer; for the person who is most controlled by his spirit will cause greater impact with his praying than the one who is moved by the soul, body or environment.

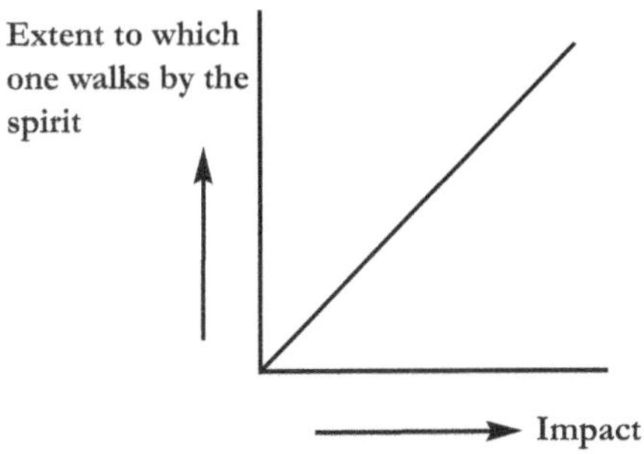

The Reletionship between The Extent to Which one Walks by the Spirit and the Impact of His Prayer

The Lord prayed thrice from the cross. The first prayer was an intercession for those who betrayed and crucified Him. He was in deepest physical agony; yet He refused to be ruled by pain. He refused to be caught up with His own needs. He refused to just wish. He actually prayed to God. He prayed for His enemies at the point of His greatest anguish. This is wonderful! Nails were driven through Him. All was totally uncomfortable. He was in immeasurable pain; yet His priority remained what it always was prayer!

That the Lord made prayer the one thing that had to be done on the cross tells us that He has demonstrated that every time is prayer time.

Let it never be said of you and me that there was a situation under which we could not pray. Let it never be said of you or me that there was a situation in which we were too tired to pray. Let it never be said of us that there was a situation in which we were in too much pain to pray. Let it never be said of you and me that there was a situation under which we were too depressed to pray. By praying on the cross, the Lord has established that men ought to pray.

- at every moment,
- in every situation,
- at all costs.

This is the only way to show that we have learnt the lesson that the Lord taught us by His praying from the cross for the forgiveness of His enemies!

The Lord's eyes were ever turned towards the Father. They were ever turned towards the needs of others. They were ever turned towards the need of people to be forgiven. They always led to prayer!

THE LAST WORDS FROM THE CROSS

The last words from the cross were a prayer. He began His stay on the cross in prayer and He ended it in prayer. How great our Saviour is! How He took prayer to heart! How He understood the importance of prayer! How He translated His understanding into action! How He prayed!

"Lord, God, Your Exalted Son prayed all through His life. He poured Himself out unceasingly to You in prayer. Even when He felt the pangs of separation from You that was caused by our sin which He bore, He never looked elsewhere but turned to You and asked why You had abandoned Him. Lord, change my life. Lord, change my heart. Make me like Him. Draw me to Yourself. Draw all Yours unto Yourself. Teach us to pray. Keep us praying. Weld our hearts to Yours and compel us to be where we ought to be in prayer. Lord, do this and then we shall be different. Lord, do this and we shall begin to be like the Lord Jesus. Lord, thank You that You are committed to doing it and You will do it. Amen."

36

PRAYING, FROM THE THRONE! FROM HIS GLORY!

"*The former priests were many in number, because they were prevented by death from continuing in office; but he holds his priesthood permanently, because he continues for ever. Consequently, he is able for all time to save those who draw near to God through him, since he always lives to make intercession for them*" (Hebrews 7:23-25).

We saw that the Lord Jesus spent the first twelve years of His life learning to pray. Then we saw that He spent the next eighteen years praying His ministry through. Thirdly, we saw that He spent as much time as possible during the three-and-a-half years of His earthly ministry in prayer. We also saw that He ended His earthly ministry on the cross with a prayer!

He finished His earthly ministry and entered into His glory, as He said, "*O foolish men, and slow of heart to believe all that the prophets have spoken! Was it not necessary that the Christ should suffer these things and enter into his glory?*" (Luke 24:25-26).

It would be expected that having laboured and having suffered, He would enter His glory to rest.

The Lord Jesus did not enter His glory to rest. He entered his glory to continue to intercede in a totally new way. On earth He interceded. On the throne He is interceding with fasting.

It is now nearly one thousand nine hundred and fifty-five years since the Lord returned to the throne and entered into His glory. It is also one thousand nine hundred and fifty-five years that have been spent by the Lord in making intercession for the saints. The Bible says that HE ALWAYS LIVES TO MAKE INTERCESSION FOR THEM! So the very purpose and the total preoccupation of the Lord on the throne is the making of intercession for the saints.

Let us look at things all over again. We can summarize them as follows:

1. Twelve years spent learning to pray.
2. Eighteen years spent praying His ministry through.
3. Three-and-a-half years spent ministering with much of it given to prayer.
4. One thousand nine hundred and fifty-five years spent interceding for the consolidation of His ministry.

We said before that He spent five years to pray through every year of His coming ministry. We also said that we are learning to do the same and should all learn to do the same. Now we see something else. He has spent 1,955 years praying for the consolidation of a 3.5-year ministry. That means that the Lord has already put 559 years of intercession for the consolidation of each year of ministry that He carried out!

If we were to derive a formula from this, we would say that 12 years of learning to pray should be followed by 18 years of praying the ministry through, which should be followed by 3.5 years of ministry, which should be followed by 1,955 years of consolidating the ministry.

We could then say that for every year of ministry a man should invest 3.5 years learning to pray, 5 years into praying through the ministry and then one year of ministry, which should be followed by 559 years of consolidation in prayer.

PRAYER IS ALL-IMPORTANT

We must evaluate the importance of prayer as is exemplified in the life of the Lord Jesus. We must endeavour to give the importance to prayer that He gave it.

The life of Jesus is an unceasing testimony to the fact that prayer is important. His life demonstrates that prayer is not only necessary, that its quality is necessary and that its quantity is necessary.

The fact that intercession for the saints is about the only thing that He is preoccupied with and that, although He has been preoccupied with it for all these 1,955 years and is continuing to pray, it means that we are committing a most dreadful sin by our superficial prayers that are short-lived. His unceasing intercession from the throne is a rebuke for the prayerlessness of the Church today. His unceasing intercession is a rebuke for the prayerlessness of individual believers. His unceasing intercession is a challenge to those who are putting a few hours of prayer into each day but who, nevertheless, think that they are doing much praying. His unceasing intercession is an invitation to all who are interested in the will of the Father to pray and to get people to pray. It is a reminder that the best thing that anyone can do for God and man is to pray, and that the best use of any time is to convert it into prayer time. His unceasing praying tells us in plain language that God cannot carry out His purpose without prayer and that, unless it is supplied to Him, He must leave many things undone that He very much wants to do.

We have said before that prayer is the rail on which the locomotive of God moves and that the more praying the saints do the more rails will be available for God and the more things God will do. The Lord Jesus is unceasingly providing the rails on which the locomotive of God is moving. Considering the prayerlessness of the Church in many quarters today, it is obvious that the work of the Lord is still continuing in our day because of the intercession of the Lord Jesus from the throne.

We have also said that fasting is the lubricating fluid that speeds the locomotive of God on its way. The Lord Jesus, by living ever to make intercession with fasting from the throne, is providing both abundant rails and abundant lubrication. What a wonderful Lord He is! How great His wonderful name is!

A LESSON FOR ALL

It is understood by some that prayer should precede an event and that prayer should be going on while the event is taking place. For example, many pray before an evangelistic campaign and many pray during the evangelistic campaign. However, the tragedy of most evangelistic campaigns is that the prayer drops or ceases completely once the campaign is over. Everyone naively expects the converts to grow without prayer and the seed to grow without being watered by abundant praying. The result of this is that many of the converts never make any progress and many that heard the gospel and were not yet saved have had the Word that they heard snatched away from them. This is because many of God's children have not come to terms with the fact that the greater and more risky work takes place after the campaign. It is then that there are many newborn babies in the Kingdom of God, and these could die if they are not taken care of.

To return to the example that we used earlier on in the book, there must be prayer so that there are spiritual pregnancies. There must be much prayer so that there are healthy spiritual births. There must also be abundant prayers that the children who are born should grow properly and healthily to maturity. Without intensive praying for the growth of those who have been born, they can die at any age, and this would be a most tragic loss. They could also become sick and, even though they do not die, they become unfruitful. The other possibility is that they could grow and become fruitful but not reach their fullest ability. This, too, is a loss. In the parable of the Sower, the seed that fell by the wayside was lost. Also lost were the seeds that fell on stony ground and on thorny ground. Of substantial loss to the farmer was that which fell on the wayside, followed by that which fell on the stony ground and then that which fell on the thorny ground. The last two had cost the farmer a lot of effort, but yielded nothing.

When we look at it from time perspective, it does not take long for a pregnancy to occur. After conception, the pregnancy takes nine months in the womb. Delivery is normally complete between one and maybe twelve hours. However, the process of growth and maturity takes very many years. The one who wants to pray things as they ought to be prayed, should pray for :

- a few minutes that the pregnancy should occur;
- nine months that the foetus should develop well.
- a few hours that delivery should be safe;
- many years that the baby should grow and become
- a healthy and useful adult.

The sad thing is that things are not being done this way and the consequences at the spiritual level are obvious.

CAREFUL PLANNING IS NECESSARY!

An evangelist ought to carefully ensure that there is much pre-campaign, during-campaign and post-campaign praying. He ought to ensure that the pre-campaign praying is of greater quantity than the during-campaign praying, and then he ought to ensure that the post-campaign praying far exceeds the pre-campaign praying in every way. In fact, many years after a campaign, intense praying ought to be going on without ceasing for those who heard the Gospel during the campaign, regardless of whether or not they were saved. It is only in this way that he can truly fulfil his ministry. Unfortunately, this is not what is being practised today. Such methods will not advance fame-hungry men before man. Such methods would place a burden on local pastors; for they would be compelled to labour much before God in prayer. Because of an unwillingness to pay the price for the post-campaign praying, they easily invite another evangelist who comes and makes some noise and the vicious cycle continues.

Anyone who wants to hear, let him hear. Such a one should look at the ministry and prayer life of the Lord Jesus and learn from it.

He should carefully ensure that there is going to be post-campaign praying for many years. If that is not guaranteed, he should organize it and ensure that the people pray and plan to continue to pray. If he finds that the people are not prepared to pay the price for post-campaign praying, he should do God honour by refusing to hold the campaign.

The same thing should apply to a minister of the Word. Each special series of messages should be preceded by much praying. This much praying should continue during the time when the Word is being ministered. Then after the Word has been preached, weeks, months and years should be invested in praying that the messages might bear the fruit that they were meant to bear in the lives of those who heard it. The faithful minister will choose the pathway of prayer, rather than the easy pathway of choosing another theme and another teacher to come and continue the dangerous routine.

May God grant us ears to hear. May He grant us hearts to obey. "Thank You, Lord Jesus, that Your example was so perfect. Help me, help us to follow it. Thank You for Your unceasing intercessions from the throne. They are the reasons why I have been able to come this far in loving You. Glory, glory be to Your name. Yes, Lord, they are the reasons why the Church has been able to come this far in loving You. Glory, glory, excellent glory be unto Your most wonderful name. Amen."

37

HIS DISCIPLES NOW!

1. You a disciple
   Of the Lord Jesus
   Your Lord learned to pray.
   He spent time praying,
   Praying to the Father
   That your faith might grow,
   Rise from sleep
   And pray like Him;
   Wrestle on your knees,
   Your Captain, the Lord Jesus Christ
   Is right now at prayer.

2. He calls to prayer
   All those who are His
   All who will follow Him
   Into conflict
   With the powers
   That hold men captive.
   Rise from ease
   Oh man, for victory.
   For to that you are called.

Labour with Him praying at night
And in the day too.

3. At the Jordan
Wrestling in prayer
He rent the heavens.
Then the Spirit
Came as a dove
And rested on Him.
He then went
In might and power
And laboured in prayer
Until the Father's gracious will
Was fully accomplished.

4. Though now on the throne
Right in His glory
He yet does one thing:
He does intercede
Praying night and day
For the saints on earth.
You are the one
For whom He has prayed
For so many years,
That you may enter right now
Into His fullness.

5. He is praying,
He is fasting,
He holds nothing back.
Arise, my brother,
Arise, my sister,
Join Him in prayer
Then the power
Of our God
Will be poured out on all.
Many will then be transformed
And then the King will come.

Yaounde, 9th July 1989

38

REND THE HEAVENS, O LORD!

Rend the heavens, O Lord!
And come down now!
Visit us afresh, O Lord!
Rend the heavens and pour Your Spirit of fire,
O God of Elijah
For this fire we pray!
So that the Church might quake at Thy presence,
To quake because of Thy awesome holy presence.

Pour down Your Spirit, O Lord!
And bend the Church!
May the Spirit of fire burn the dross,
As when fire kindles brushwood!
Arise, O Lord, and stir us to holiness,
As when fire causes water to boil!
Yea, may Your Spirit move in the Church,
To re-awaken dead consciences to repentance, restoration and consecration!
Yea, Lord, as fire causes water to boil, bring us back to holiness and truth!

Rend the heavens, O Lord!
And descend now; now in this last hour!
In this last hour of the last day!
Pour the promised Spirit of power,
And make Thy name known to Thy adversaries!
Bend the Church, O Lord!
Visit us now, visit us today!
Oh for a conscious awareness of God in the Church!
Oh for a deeper revelation of Your awesome holiness!

Yes, Lord, descend now!
And cause Thy people to tremble at Thy presence!
If there is one need now, O Lord!
It is that You may rend the heavens,
And come down now!
That the nations might tremble at Thy presence,
At the presence of the Holy One of Israel,
As when fire causes water to boil!
Revive Thy work, O Lord!
And turn away the captivity of the nations!

Rend the heavens, O Lord!
Rend some hearts, even my own heart, rend!
Oh for the heavens to be rent!
And show forth Thy terrible works to the nations!
That they may tremble at Thy presence!
Come down now, O Lord!
And melt stony hearts,

As the mountains melt as wax before You!
Bring us back to the apostolic days of old,
For that indeed is heaven on earth!

Rend some waiting hearts.
And rend the heavens!
That we may hear,
And perceive Thee by the ear,
And glorify Thy name,
As the God of gods!
Yea, in all, O Lord,
Glorify Thy name!
Come, Lord Jesus! Amen.

Bend me, O Lord!
Bend my stiff back!
Rend my heart, O Lord!
Rend this callous heart of mine!
Melt my stony heart, O Lord!
As the mountains melt as was before Thee!
Oh, that I may know the baptism of fire
To burn every dross in me,
As when fire kindles brushwood!

Bend me, O Lord!
And rend my heart!
Oh, for a heart acquainted with continuous brokenness!
Oh, for a heart acquainted with continuous contrition!

Oh, for a heart acquainted with tears,
Increasing tears, unceasing tears over my own sins!
Give me tears for revival, O Lord!
Give me passion for souls!
Give me burden for Your visitation!

Oh, for a heart acquainted with great sorrow,
unceasing sorrow over my own sins!
Oh, for a heart acquainted with unceasing anguish over my own sins!
Oh, for a heart that knows a perpetual confession and forsaking of sins!
Oh, for a heart that knows increasing tears, unceasing tears as an intercessor!
Oh, for a heart that knows great sorrow, unceasing sorrow as an intercessor!
Oh, for a heart that knows unceasing anguish as an intercessor,
For the five billion souls on planet Earth!

Bend me, O Lord!
Rend my heart, I pray Thee!
Oh, for a heart that knows the Lordship of the Spirit of intercession!
Oh, for a heart to bear God's burdens with the Spirit of intercession!
Oh, for a heart that really prays and prays with words known!
Oh, for a heart that really prays and prays with words unknown!
Oh, for a heart that groans with the Spirit of intercession!
Oh, for a heart that sighs, deeply sighs to discharge God's bur-

dens!
Oh, for a heart that knows unceasing tears, tears for souls!
Oh, for a heart that knows great sorrow, unceasing sorrow for souls!
Oh, for a heart that knows unceasing anguish, great anguish for souls!
Bend me, O Lord, and give me such a heart!
Rend my heart to meet this need!

Am I an intercessor?
I am greatly limited and inadequate!
Oh, that I could become an intercessor indeed!
Oh, that I could intercede indeed!
Bend me, O Lord!
To become an intercessor as those of old!
You did this bending work in them; do it in me, Lord!
Bend us, O Lord! And give us intercessors!
Bend us and save the world!
Bend us and bring back apostolic days now,
For that indeed is heaven on earth!
O Lord, rend the heavens and come down now!
Come, Lord! Amen.

Donald NGONGE
28th August 1998

VERY IMPORTANT

If you have not yet received Jesus as your Lord and Saviour, I encourage you to receive Him. Here are some steps to help you,

ADMIT that you are a sinner by nature and by practice and that on your own you are without hope. Tell God you have personally sinned against Him in your thoughts, words and deeds. Confess your sins to Him, one after another in a sincere prayer. Do not leave out any sins that you can remember. Truly turn from your sinful ways and abandon them. If you stole, steal no more. If you have been committing adultery or fornication, stop it. God will not forgive you if you have no desire to stop sinning in all areas of your life, but if you are sincere, He will give you the power to stop sinning.

BELIEVE that Jesus Christ, who is God's Son, is the only Way, the only Truth and the only Life. Jesus said, "*I am the way, the truth and the life; no one comes to the Father, but by me*" (John 14:6). The Bible says, "*For there is one God, and there is one mediator between God and men, the man Christ Jesus, who gave himself as a ransom for all*" (1 Timothy 2:5-6). "*And there is salvation in no one else (apart from Jesus), for there is no other name under heaven given among men by which we must be saved*" (Acts 4:12). "*But to all who received him, who believed in his name, he gave power to become children of God...*" (John 1:12). But,

CONSIDER the cost of following Him. Jesus said that all who follow Him must deny themselves, and this includes selfish financial, social and other interests. He also wants His followers to take up their crosses and follow Him. Are you prepared to abandon your own interests daily for those of Christ? Are you prepared to be led in a new direction by Him? Are you prepared to suffer for Him and die for Him if need be? Jesus will have nothing to do with half-hearted people. His demands are total. He will only receive and forgive those who are prepared to follow Him AT ANY COST. Think about it and count the cost. If you are prepared to follow Him, come what may, then there is something to do.

INVITE Jesus to come into your heart and life. He says, "*Behold I stand at the door and knock. If anyone hears my voice and opens the door (to his heart and life), I will come in to him and eat with him, and he with me* " (Revelation 3:20). Why don't you pray a prayer like the following one or one of your own construction as the Holy Spirit leads ?

> "Lord Jesus, I am a wretched, lost sinner who has sinned in thought, word and deed. Forgive all my sins and cleanse me. Receive me, Saviour and transform me into a child of God. Come into my heart now and give me eternal life right now. I will follow you at all costs, trusting the Holy Spirit to give me all the power I need."

When you pray this prayer sincerely, Jesus answers at once and justifies you before God and makes you His child.

Please write to me and I will pray for you and help you as you go on with Jesus Christ...

If you have received the Lord Jesus-Christ after reading this book, please write to us at the following addresse :

For Europe :

Editions du Livre Chrétien

4, Rue du Révérend Père Cloarec

92400 Courbevoie

Courriel : editionlivrechretien@gmail.com

ABOUT THE AUTHOR

Professor Z.T. Fomum was born in 1945 in Cameroon and was taken to be with the Lord on the 14th March 2009. He was admitted to the Bachelor of Science degree, graduating as a prize-winning student from Fourah Bay College in the University of Sierra Leone. His research in Organic Chemistry earned him a Ph.D. degree in the University of Makerere, Kampala, Uganda. Recently, his published scientific work was evaluated and found to be of high distinction, earning him the award of a Doctor of Science degree from the University of Durham in Great Britain. As a Professor of Organic Chemistry in the University of Yaoundé I, Cameroon, he supervised and co-supervised more than 100 Master's and Doctoral degree theses. He published with others over 160 scientific articles in leading international journals.

The author read over 1350 books on the Christian Faith and wrote over 150 titles to advance the Gospel of Christ. 4 million copies of these books are in circulation in 11 languages, as well as 16 million gospel tracts in 17 languages. In pursuance of the purpose to proclaim the Gospel of Jesus Christ, he also made a total of over 700 missionary journeys in Cameroon and over 500 in 70 nations. These ranged from 2 days to 6 weeks in all the world's six continents.

The author led a Church-planting and missionary-sending movement, by whose ministrations, more than 10,000 healing miracles were performed by God in answer to prayer in the name of Jesus.

These miracles include instant healings of; headaches, cancers, HIV/AIDS, blindness, deafness, dumbness, paralysis, madness and diverse diseases.

The author was married to Prisca Zei Fomum and they had 7 children who are all actively involved in serving the Lord. Prisca is a national and international minister specialising in the winning and discipling of children to Jesus Christ. She also communicates and imparts the vision of the ministry to children, with a view to raise and build up ministers for them.

The author owed all that he was and all that God had done in him and through him, to the unmerited favours and blessings of God and to his world wide army of friends and co-workers. He considered himself nothing without them and the blessings of God, and would have amounted to nothing but for them.

May the Lord receive all the glory!

Cet ouvrage a été imprimé
en septembre 2014 par

CPI

FIRMIN-DIDOT

27650 Mesnil-sur-l'Estrée
N° d'impression : 124301
Dépôt légal : septembre 2014

Imprimé en France